EUROPE: IN OR OUT?

EUROPE: IN OR OUT?
Everything You Need to Know

———————

DAVID CHARTER

Biteback Publishing

This updated edition published in Great Britain in 2016 by
Biteback Publishing Ltd
Westminster Tower
3 Albert Embankment
London SE1 7SP
Copyright © David Charter 2014, 2016

ISBN 978-1-78590-041-9

10 9 8 7 6 5 4 3 2 1

A CIP catalogue record for this book is available from the British Library.

Set in Sabon

Printed and bound in Great Britain by
CPI Group (UK) Ltd, Croydon CR0 4YY

For my parents, with love

CONTENTS

INTRODUCTION

'This is perhaps the most important decision the British people will have to take at the ballot box in our lifetimes.'

With these words, David Cameron introduced his detailed plans for a referendum on Britain's membership of the European Union. He set out four main goals for a renegotiation of Britain's relationship with its nearest neighbours ahead of the momentous vote. Ten years after he called on his fellow Conservatives to stop 'banging on about Europe', the referendum on whether to remain or leave was dominating the government's domestic and international agenda. This book looks at the main aspects of Britain's dealings with the 28-nation organisation, the achievements and the aggravations, and asks in each case what it would mean to walk away. The pros and cons are explained in ten themes including democracy, prosperity and sovereignty, and in ten sectors where the EU most impacts everyday life in Britain such as finance, farming and fishing. In his speech in November 2015, delivered at Chatham House in London, Cameron made clear that if he judged his renegotiation to be a success, he would campaign 'with all my heart and all my soul' to keep Britain inside a reformed European Union. This would be 'unambiguously in our national interest'. The Prime Minister said that the central reason for continued engagement with the EU was 'security' – both economic and national. This marked an important evolution of his approach from the speech almost three years earlier in which he announced he would hold a referendum on the EU if the Conservatives won power in 2015. Speaking at the Bloomberg financial news agency in London in January 2013, it was the Single Market that formed his core reason for staying in the EU and security was mentioned just twice. But in the Chatham House speech, which mentioned security thirty-one times, he argued that the worsening global security picture also made a strong argument for EU membership:

In 2015, our membership of the European Union is not just a matter of trade and commerce, of pounds and pence. It is about our national security as well as our economic security. The world is undoubtedly a more dangerous place than when I made my speech at Bloomberg three years ago. Then, ISIL didn't exist. Now it controls substantial territory in Iraq and Syria and directly threatens our country. Then, Ukraine was at peace. Now it is in crisis, after Russia invaded Crimea and Eastern Ukraine. And of course the war in Syria has unleashed a wave of migration towards Europe which we see night after night on our television screens. Britain has never joined the Schengen border-free zone, so we retain our border controls. This, and our geographical status as an island, means we are less directly affected than other European countries by this crisis. Our agreement with France, as a fellow EU member, means that our main border control with continental Europe effectively operates now at Calais, not Dover. And our decision to admit 20,000 Syrian refugees from the camps was a British national sovereign decision. But our membership of the EU does matter for our national security and for the security of our allies, which is one reason why our friends in the world strongly urge us to remain in the EU.

It was a powerful argument. Three days later it was undermined in the most spectacular and appalling fashion when terrorists killed 130 people in a series of coordinated attacks in Paris. Over the following days, it emerged that several of the attackers had travelled from Syria, using the massive influx of migrants into Europe as cover. Of the suicide bombers who struck at the Stade de France, two used fake Syrian passports to enter Greece in October 2015, while the third was known to be fighting in Syria but had somehow slipped back. All the terrorists were able to move freely around the continent thanks to the Schengen system of open borders between twenty-six countries, which abolished internal passport checks. Despite Cameron's point that Britain had retained its border controls by staying out of Schengen, it was not only the Belgian authorities that Paris ringleader Abdelhamid Abaaoud had evaded after being sentenced to jail in absentia in his native Belgium for earlier terrorist activity. A phone belonging to him was found to contain photographs of locations in Birmingham and it was discovered that he travelled by ferry to the UK a few months before the Paris attacks to meet fellow jihadists. Questioned on this security lapse in the House of Commons, Theresa May, the Home Secretary, refused to comment on individual cases. Nevertheless, security remains Cameron's central argument for EU membership. He explained in his Chatham House speech that the EU amplifies Britain's ability to act on the world stage:

> The EU, like NATO and our membership of the UN Security Council, is a tool that a British Prime Minister uses to get things done in the world and protect our country. When Russia invaded Ukraine, and European leaders met, it was Britain that pushed through sanctions to penalise Russia and ensure a robust response. On Iran, it was Britain that helped impose the tough sanctions which got Iran to the negotiating table. These things were done through the EU. The point I am making is this – if the British Prime Minister was no longer present at European summits, we would lose that voice and therefore permanently change our ability to get things done in the world.

Yet Cameron put this position at risk himself, even though he never really wanted to have a referendum at all.

The Prime Minister was pushed into announcing it by a large group of eurosceptic MPs in his own ranks, as well as by pressure from the media and a popular mood of disenchantment with the EU that saw a dramatic increase in support for the UK Independence Party, a political party founded to campaign for British with-drawal from Brussels. The rise of UKIP was not just down to anger at Europe, although this was the reason it was formed at the time of the Maastricht Treaty which created the European Union. UKIP also thrived on popular concern at high levels of immigration and discontent with a political class that seemed out of touch with parts of the electorate. Many Conservative Party MPs felt that a referendum on EU membership would be a good way of pleasing their grass roots as well as neutralising UKIP's appeal in the run-up to the 2015 general election. A referendum could also win support from voters across the political spectrum who had not had a say on Britain's relationship with Europe for four decades.

Labour refused to match Cameron's referendum promise. But in 1975 it was the Labour government of Harold Wilson that set the precedent with the country's first ballot on Europe, when the UK decided by an overwhelming two to one to stay in the European Economic Community (EEC), the forerunner of today's EU. In the depths of the Cold War and with Britain plagued by high inflation and the Three-Day Week, there was a powerful case for linking up with our continental allies. Much has changed since then. Globalisation, the fall of Communism and the emergence of developing powers like Brazil, China and India have given Britain a range of international economic options unimaginable in the 1970s. The EEC itself has been transformed, most notably by the Maastricht Treaty of 1993 that turned it into the European Union and set up the euro.

The six-nation group expanded to nine members when the UK joined in 1973 along with Denmark and Ireland, and the organisation kept growing, with the historic enlargements of 2004, 2007 and 2013 bringing eleven former Iron Curtain countries into the club. Britain was the driving force behind both the expansion and the creation of the Single Market in the 1980s which entailed abandoning the right to veto European laws in many policy areas. Further concessions of national sovereignty were made to extend EU legislative power over employment and social conditions, as well as judicial and police cooperation. The Lisbon Treaty of 2009 added the European External Action Service – the EU's own version of the Foreign Office – with branches in almost every country of the world. Public consent for these steps towards broader and deeper continental integration was never sought in a referendum – although Ireland held popular votes every time a major treaty transferred new powers to Brussels.

Frustration among the public, politicians and the media grew as the referendum option was seemingly promised by British political leaders only to be cancelled or avoided. Tony Blair said that there would be a public vote on the proposed EU Constitution in 2005, only to call it off after the French and Dutch had both voted against the document and effectively sent it back to the drawing board. Most of the proposed changes were repackaged into the Lisbon Treaty but the Labour government under Gordon Brown refused to put it to a referendum, arguing that there was no tradition for a public vote on a treaty that simply updated EU rules. Labour's argument was undermined when Valéry Giscard d'Estaing, the former French President who oversaw the drafting of the ill-fated Constitution, welcomed the Lisbon Treaty by declaring: 'The text is, in fact, a rerun of a great part of the substance of the Constitutional Treaty.' In an article in *The Sun* newspaper in 2007, David Cameron, while Leader of the Opposition, said: 'Today I will give this cast-iron guarantee: if I become PM a Conservative government will hold a referendum on any EU treaty that emerges from these negotiations.' Two years later, after the Czech Republic became the final EU country to ratify the Lisbon Treaty, Cameron, still in opposition, abandoned his referendum pledge. The changes were 'set in legal cement ... sadly our battle to stop this EU treaty has come to an end', he said.

David Cameron instinctively felt that a fight over Europe would be a diversion from his core tasks as Prime Minister. That is why he told the Conservatives' annual conference in 2006 that the party needed to drop its obsession with the EU.

> For too long, instead of talking about the things that most people care about, we talked about what we cared about most. While parents worried about childcare, getting the kids to school, balancing work and family life, we were banging on about Europe.

That warning seems a long time ago now. In the same article in which he dropped his cast-iron guarantee of a referendum on the Lisbon Treaty, he admitted the real reason why he did not want to bang on about the EU: 'The to-do list for the next government is long and daunting. That is why I know that if we win that election, we cannot afford to waste time having a row with Europe.' For Cameron, Europe was not a core issue. It was a time waster. Many in his party felt differently, however, and bit by bit he was pushed into the position of announcing a referendum, even if his coalition with the pro-EU Liberal Democrats meant that he could only deliver it once re-elected in 2015 with a Conservative majority. Cameron said that he needed time for a renegotiation of the UK's terms of membership before a public vote by the end of 2017. The reason to play for time was clear – opinion polls suggested that an immediate in/out referendum would be too close to call, while a successful renegotiation could win round decisive numbers of voters.

Cameron's renegotiation was based around the four policy areas of economic governance, competitiveness, sovereignty and immigration which he believed would address the concerns of many voters, and which he set out in his Chatham House speech:

Objective 1: protect the Single Market for Britain and others outside the Eurozone.

What I mean by that is a set of binding principles that guarantee fairness between Euro and non-Euro countries.

Objective 2: write competitiveness into the DNA of the whole European Union. And this includes cutting the total burden on business.

Objective 3: exempt Britain from an 'ever closer union' and bolster national parliaments. Not through warm words but through legally binding and irreversible changes.

And objective 4: tackle abuses of the right to free movement, and enable us to control migration from the European Union, in line with our manifesto.

The fine print of the four goals was subject to intense diplomacy by British officials and individual meetings Cameron held with the heads of the other twenty-seven member states. The most delicate changes were boosting the power of national parliaments and disapplying the EU's commitment to 'ever closer union', as discussed in this book's chapters on Democracy and Sovereignty, and attempting to reduce the 'pull factor' of welfare payments by stopping child benefit payments from being sent overseas and banning EU migrants from in-work benefits for four years, as discussed in the Immigration chapter. For some in his own party, the entire renegotiation was not ambitious enough, while others argued that it would change Britain's relationship to protect it from the continental goal of political union. There were some things that were simply not up for discussion, however, such as the principle of free movement of people – regarded as one of the founding principles of the Single Market. Even if Britain were to leave the EU, it could still find itself subject to the freedom of movement of EU citizens from the twenty-seven other member countries. That is because if an independent Britain wanted to retain full trading relations with the EU, it could follow non-EU member Norway into the European Economic Area. This special category, also used by Iceland and tiny Liechtenstein, allows full access to the Single Market but requires acceptance of its 'four freedoms' of the movement of capital, goods, services and people, without allowing any decisive say over how the rules are set.

The referendum exposed a lack of clear vision about what should be the UK's precise future relationship with the EU among some who wanted to see a Brexit (British exit). If not the Norway option, should an independent Britain go back to the European Free Trade Association, which it originally helped to form in 1960 as an alternative to the EEC, and seek a series of bilateral policy agreements with the EU like Switzerland, even though the Swiss financial services sector does not enjoy complete access to the Single Market? Or should it settle for a Free Trade Agreement like a more distant partner such as South Korea or Canada? UKIP and other campaigners for Brexit were very good at harnessing anger at the interference of the EU in everyday British life but not so good at explaining what would really happen if Britain left. The chapters of this book on the sectors most affected by the EU relationship will assess the impact of the various ways of leaving the club described above.

This book can be used as a scorecard to weigh up membership and assess whether it still works for Britain, although none of the topics exists in isolation and there are many areas of overlap. Not all the subjects will carry equal weight when it comes to judging the best path for Britain to follow. For some voters, the fate of British sovereignty will be far more important than the impact upon life in the City of London, while for others concerned above all about the country's balance sheet, the opposite might be the case. Nor is Britain's relationship with the EU a static one. It has changed dramatically over four decades of membership and it will keep on changing, not least as the nineteen countries in the single currency share more of their economic sovereignty to shore up the euro.

I worked for five years in Brussels covering the EU for *The Times* before moving to Berlin to report on Germany. I confess to approaching the EU from a sceptical viewpoint – a journalistic scepticism of any system of government which spends billions of pounds of taxpayers' money. I have endeavoured to analyse the facts and test the arguments of those trying to persuade us one way or the other to stay or to leave the EU. My first book *Au Revoir, Europe,* published in December 2012, looked at how Britain reached the point of departure from the European club. This book, fully revised and updated for this second edition after it was first published in 2014, contains the essential information and arguments for assessing what is best for Britain when it comes to deciding on Europe: in or out?

THEMES

DEMOCRACY

IN Britain, like every EU member state, has one appointed European Commissioner and one judge at the European Court of Justice. It has seventy-three out of 751 elected Members of the European Parliament (MEPs). Ministers who take decisions in meetings of the European Council must win allies to get their way under Qualified Majority Voting but have a veto in some sensitive areas like treaty change, tax, defence and foreign policy.

OUT Britain will regain control over EU policy areas but companies trading in Europe will still have to abide by standards and rules set in Brussels with no representation from UK ministers or MEPs. If the UK wants to stay in the Single Market, it must follow all the laws on the free movement of capital, goods, people and services without having a vote on them.

KEY STATS Britain's voice in the European Parliament diminished from 18.2 per cent of MEPs to 9.7 per cent as more nations joined the EU. It has the joint third highest number of MEPs with Italy after Germany (ninety-six) and France (seventy-four). Turnout in the 2014 European Parliament elections was 35.6 per cent in the UK compared to 66.1 per cent in the 2015 general election.

One week a month, the 751 Members of the European Parliament (MEPs), up to 2,000 staff and all their paperwork make the 250-mile trip from their offices in Brussels to their other offices in Strasbourg. Under the Treaty of Amsterdam, agreed by Sir John Major and ratified under Tony Blair, the European Parliament must meet twelve times a year in the capital of Alsace, a

German-speaking region of France chosen to symbolise the post-war reconciliation between Europe's two great foes. But because the parliament has a summer holiday and does not sit in August, the whole travelling circus by road, train and plane must take place on two separate occasions in October to make up the dozen sessions 'of equal duration' enshrined in EU law. The whole exercise costs at least €180 million a year, meaning that the European Parliament's seven-year budget for 2014–20 has set aside £1 billion for shuttling back and forth between its two homes.[4] And when the European Parliament moves, the twenty-eight members of the European Commission also hold their weekly 'college' meeting in Strasbourg, accompanied by their key staff. 'The current arrangements are indefensible – ludicrously expensive and impractical. And one of the best adverts for EU waste,' said David Lidington, the UK's Minister for Europe. Roland Ries, the mayor of Strasbourg, has a different view: 'The legitimacy of Strasbourg is derived not only from law but, more importantly, from history. As a city that symbolises Franco-German reconciliation, it is the European capital of peace, democracy and human rights.' Holding the parliament full time in Brussels would save 19,000 tonnes of CO_2 a year, which would contribute to EU emissions targets.[5] MEPs voted in 2011 to merge two of the sessions to save a bit of money but this was immediately challenged at the European Court of Justice by the governments of France and Luxembourg (the Grand Duchy hosts a third site of the European Parliament, its secretariat employing

2,432 officials). The court ruled in favour of France and Luxembourg. Then in November 2013, the democratically elected MEPs voted by 483 to 141 to base the parliament in a single location. It was a symbolic gesture. A treaty agreement can only be changed by the unanimous agreement of all member states and France would assuredly veto any attempt to end Strasbourg's special status.

Even though the European Parliament has gained new powers to amend laws with every treaty that has been passed over the last four decades, its impotence in deciding where it actually meets shows that true power in the EU machine still lies elsewhere. The member states, whose ministers and leaders meet in the European Council, remain more powerful where decisions must be made by unanimity. But their agenda is usually set by the body that proposes EU legislation – the European Commission, made up of an elite cadre of civil servants and overseen by twenty-eight nationally appointed commissioners, giving it a uniquely important role. A fourth institution, the European Court of Justice, with one appointed judge from each member state, has also become a law-making power through its many judgments over the years that have not just clarified but extended legislation. These are the four main bodies contributing to the making of EU law in a complicated system often criticised for suffering from a 'democratic deficit' and, whether the MEPs are sitting in Brussels or Strasbourg, being remote from voters.

The democratic deficit accusation partly stems from

a lack of direct consultation on the relentless development of the EU with ordinary voters who feel that they should have been offered a say through a referendum on some of the important changes, such as the creation of the European Union itself in 1993 from its predecessor, the European Community. It also arises from the system of law-making in Brussels that is hard to follow and not well understood. Senior EU figures are very touchy about claims that they lack democratic accountability, however. José Manuel Barroso, President of the European Commission from 2004 to 2014, used to say that he was doubly democratic because first he was elected as Prime Minister of Portugal and then he was 'elected' by the other European leaders (possibly the world's smallest constituency) to be head of the EU's bureaucracy. Every country appoints a member of the European Commission and usually it is someone who has held high political office. The two most recent British commissioners, Baroness Ashton of Upholland and Baron Hill of Oareford, had both been Leader of the House of Lords, although they were never elected to parliament, having been created life peers.

But democracy can be in the eye of the beholder. It is worth pointing out that none of the 750 or so members of the House of Lords has been elected to the chamber by the public and ninety-two hereditary Lords remain on the red benches. So the UK, with its hereditary head of state, could also be said to suffer from a democratic deficit because the House of Lords has an important role in revising legislation, although the main offices of government are usually held by MPs from the elected House of Commons. The European Parliament was created to add a democratic element to a bureaucratic EU system. When Britain joined in 1973, it was a European Assembly, with thirty-six British members seconded directly from the House of Commons and House of Lords. In 1979, it held its first direct elections. Across the EU, turnout has decreased at every subsequent election from 62 per cent in 1979 to 42.6 per cent in 2014 (in the UK it actually went up slightly from 34.7 per cent to 35.6 per cent) suggesting that voters feel detached from a body that is poorly reported in the British media and only has the right to revise, not to propose, legislation. Few MEPs have significant recognition in Britain and it has been used as a training ground for up-and-coming Westminster politicians like Nick Clegg, who was an MEP from 1999 to 2004. The EU's own Eurobarometer poll for spring 2015 found that only 61 per cent of British respondents even knew that Members of the European Parliament were directly elected.

As the EU has more than tripled in membership since 1973 from nine to twenty-eight nations, Britain's relative ability to influence its decisions has steadily declined – another factor in the perceived democratic deficit. The UK, especially under Tony Blair, was a champion of recruiting more Eastern European countries but the result was a reduction of Britain's voting strength in the European Council from 17.2 to 8.4 per cent and in the European Parliament from 18.2 per cent of MEPs to 9.7 per cent. Even more worrying from the point of view of British influence has been the sharp drop in British officials working in the EU institutions. In 2014, only two candidates from the UK passed the tough entrance exams to work at the EU compared to fifteen from France and sixteen from Germany. While Britain has 12.3 per cent of the EU population, the proportion of UK staff at the European Commission – the body that proposes and monitors EU laws – was down to just 4.3 per cent in 2015 compared to 8.3 per cent from Germany and 9.7 per cent from France.[6] Even Poland, which only joined the EU in 2004, supplied 4.9 per cent of EU staff. It was another aspect of Britain's growing alienation from Brussels. Bright graduates are either put off from working there by their inability to speak foreign languages or by the poor image of the EU as a place to build their careers.

Various plans have been suggested to try and address the EU's democratic deficit and to help it connect with voters. One was dreamed up by MEPs to try to boost voter turnout in the 2014 European Parliament elections – each political group agreed to nominate one prominent politician as their candidate for President of the European Commission. The theory was that linking the campaign to recognisable figures would inspire voters. There were a couple of obvious flaws in the argument – the first was the choice of uninspiring figures little known outside their own country and the second was the fact that much more recognisable figures currently running national governments were reluctant to be named as candidates for an EU position while supposedly staying focused on their day job. 'Opponents see a vote for a Commission President via the parliament as illusory, misleading and irrelevant,' wrote *The Guardian*. 'Will a Swede vote liberal because of a Flemish contender? Or a Greek vote social democrat in support of a German? ... Or will all of them vote because of what they perceive to be going on in their own countries and politics?' In the event, most of the big political groups in the European Parliament did nominate a so-called 'Spitzenkandidat' and when the main centre-right alliance won the most seats, their top candidate Jean-Claude Juncker became the next President of the European Commission. A precedent was set for a more direct democratic mechanism for the choice of president but, as a way of boosting turnout, it was a flop. The number of voters in 2014 was down slightly on the 43 per cent recorded in 2009.

Another plan proposed by senior German politicians was to hold a direct Europe-wide election for the post of EU President, a combined role to run both the European Commission and European Council. This could see hustings held by two or three rivals in every country and would create a figure with a very powerful personal mandate to lead the EU, much like an American President. The extra authority that this would bestow on such a person makes it likely that Britain would block the proposal, as it has done in the past – not least because it would appear like a move towards a United States of Europe. That is the core issue with some of the plans to enhance the EU's direct democratic accountability – they also tend to increase its power.

Besides, voters have drifted away from European Parliament elections over the years even though more responsibility has steadily been given to MEPs. It is national parliaments that should be given more say over EU legislation, according to an idea first floated by William Hague while Foreign Secretary to extend the little-used 'yellow card' for MPs to send legislation back to the European Commission for further consideration. 'Trust in the institutions is at an all-time low. The EU is facing a crisis of legitimacy,' Hague told a conference in Germany in May 2013.

> We should explore whether the yellow card provision could be strengthened or extended to give our parliaments the right to ask the Commission to start again where legislation is too intrusive, and fails the proportionality test. And we should think about going further still and consider a red card to give national parliaments the right to block legislation that need not be agreed at the European level.

The 'yellow card' was introduced by the Lisbon Treaty in 2009 but is viewed as weak because it only allows national parliaments to ask the Commission to 'reconsider' a proposal. The rules also allow only eight weeks to reach the requisite total of one third of national parliaments objecting to a particular European Commission proposal. Partly because of these onerous conditions, it was only used twice up until the end of 2015. In the first case, the Commission withdrew its proposal, which sought to place limits on the right to strike, but in the second case, on the proposed European Public Prosecutor, the Commission decided to go ahead regardless, despite the opposition of eleven national parliaments. This prompted the Fresh Start group of Conservative MPs, which campaign to curtail EU powers, to propose that 'a real game changer for democratic accountability' would be for a red card to apply to existing rules and not just new proposals.

> This would at last provide a mechanism for national parliaments to tackle existing, poor legislation and would provide a permanent means to reverse the ongoing EU power-grab. The Dutch Parliament recently proposed a similar mechanism. A red card on existing legislation should trigger a one-year sunset clause after which the legislation would expire unless particular member states decide to retain it under enhanced cooperation among themselves.

The EU, however, relies upon all member states agreeing to honour past agreements – even when the governments that made those agreements change. Nevertheless, David Cameron made a form of 'red card' for national parliaments a key part of his renegotiation ahead of the referendum. He did not seek retrospective powers to throw out existing laws but the right to block future proposals, explaining in his letter to Donald Tusk, President of the European Council: 'I want to enhance the role of national parliaments, by proposing a new arrangement where groups of national parliaments, acting together, can stop unwanted legislative proposals.' Tusk proposed a red card could be shown to new EU legislation provided at least 55 per cent of parliaments agreed within a twelve-week period. This did not go as far as some of Cameron's own MPs wanted. Ninety-five of them were said to have signed a private letter in January 2014 calling for national parliaments to have the individual right of a red card veto over EU laws. William Hague spelled out why giving single parliaments the right of veto was incompatible with membership of the EU:

> If parliaments all around the EU were regularly and unilaterally able to choose which bits of EU law they would apply and which bits they would not, the European Single Market would not work and even a Swiss-style free trade arrangement with the EU would not work.

It was a sign of how strongly the ninety-five Conservative MPs felt about returning the UK Parliament's democratic supremacy that they proposed a measure which would wreck the Single Market created by Margaret Thatcher, seen as the most important part of the EU by other Conservatives.

Leaving the EU would not necessarily resolve the democratic deficit felt by many in Britain. Under one scenario, it could even get worse. An option for Britain if it took the democratic decision in a referendum to leave the EU would be to follow non-members Norway, Iceland and Liechtenstein into the European Economic Area (EEA) to preserve full access to the Single Market. Unlike full EU members, the EEA countries make their own policies on farming, fishing, justice, overseas trade and regional funding but are duty bound to accept every EU law relating to the four freedoms – the movement of capital, goods, people and services – that underpin the Single Market. That includes accepting all the EU's social and employment legislation along with state aid, competition and consumer protection laws which are regarded by Brussels as integral to the Single Market system, as well as many of its environmental laws. As an EU member, Britain has been able to block the full force of the EU Working Time Directive by finding allies to support an opt-out from its 48-hour week. If Britain left the EU, the blocking alliance could crumble, leaving the UK legally required to implement the directive in full if it joined the EEA to stay inside the Single Market. Open Europe has estimated the annual extra cost to employers of losing the opt-out at between £9.2 billion and £11.9 billion a year.[7] The EEA members also accept the free movement of workers on the same basis as EU members and with the same access to national welfare systems.

An independent review for the Norwegian government concluded in 2012 that a democratic deficit was inevitable if Norway took part in the Single Market but not the EU:

The most problematic aspect of Norway's form of association with the EU is the fact that Norway is in practice
bound to adopt EU policies and rules on a broad range
of issues without being a member and without voting
rights. This raises democratic problems. Norway is not
represented in decision-making processes that have direct
consequences for Norway, and neither do we have any
significant influence on them. Moreover, our form of
association with the EU dampens political engagement
and debate in Norway and makes it difficult to monitor
the Government and hold it accountable in its European
policy. This is not surprising; the democratic deficit is a
well-known aspect of the EEA Agreement that has been
there from the start. It is the price Norway pays for
enjoying the benefits of European integration without
being a member of the organisation that is driving these
developments.

Norway's Conservative Prime Minister, Erna Solberg,
warned Britain against following her country into the
EEA relationship with the EU. Ahead of talks with
Cameron in 2014, she said:

I don't believe that Great Britain, with its old empire
mind-set, should consider becoming a member of an
organisation which basically means that laws and rules
which are made in other countries are implemented
directly. I think those in the British debate who look
at Norway's association underestimate how closely

connected we actually are with many of the laws and rules they are annoyed with.

Switzerland also refused to join the EU and rejected the EEA in a referendum in 1992 to stay in the European Free Trade Association (EFTA) outside the Single Market. It has a Free Trade Agreement for goods but not for services, and has agreed around 200 technical bilateral agreements on different aspects of cooperation, from research to transport. Nevertheless, it effectively adopts large swathes of EU law to maintain its strong trading links (62.8 per cent of total Swiss trade was with the EU in 2014[8]) and its involvement in the Schengen borderless travel zone which means Switzerland has done away with passport checks for those entering from the EU. 'In order to make its economy as EU-compatible as possible, Switzerland has adopted a policy of "voluntary adaptation" whereby Swiss law is aligned with the EU's acquis communautaire [body of law],' said the Centre for Swiss Politics at the University of Kent, in a paper for MPs' Foreign Affairs Select Committee.

Recent research shows that around 55 per cent of the laws passed by the Swiss parliament concern transposition of international, including EU, law. The bilateral treaties and the country's voluntary adaptation have led to Switzerland being much more deeply integrated with the EU than suggested by its formal status as a non-member. Indeed, in certain respects such integration is deeper than that of EU members such as the UK, as the case of Schengen shows.

The Swiss system offers a more democratic solution than the Norwegian model because all new laws are scrutinised by its parliament, although many are of EU origin. Switzerland does retain, on paper at least, full legal decision-making powers over the laws it passes. It does not fall under the jurisdiction of the European Court of Justice. Another attraction of the Swiss model for those who want Britain to withdraw from the EU is the fact that it does not have to implement Single Market legislation relating to social and employment law.

Senior figures in the EU are painfully aware that they are regarded as remote, unrecognised and undemocratic. Precisely a quarter of British people told the spring 2015 Eurobarometer poll that they had not heard of the European Commission and 16 per cent said they had not heard of the European Parliament. In both cases, these were by far the highest levels of ignorance of all twenty-eight EU member nations. If nothing else, it was an indictment of schools, the media and politicians themselves for failing to communicate the basic structures of the EU.

Faced with growing levels of discontent across the EU, the Lisbon Treaty proposed a measure called the European Citizens' Initiative to try and make a direct connection with voters. This requires the European Commission to consider proposing legislation if called upon by a petition signed by at least one million people from at least one quarter of the member states. It was partly inspired by the earlier petition to end the European Parliament's travelling circus, which gained 1.27 million signatures (although it has not yet achieved its aim). Introduced in 2012, by the end of 2015 there had been more than fifty attempts to raise a petition for a new EU law, but only three made it through the vetting and signature collection process to receive a formal response from the European Commission. The successful initiatives called for 'water as a human right', a ban on human embryo research and an end to animal vivisection. None resulted in new legislation, although the first was taken into account during a review of the EU's Drinking Water Directive. One of the initiatives rejected by the European Commission, a petition to stop the proposed EU trade deal with the US, received more than 3.2 million signatures.

György Schöpflin, a Hungarian Member of the European Parliament and author of a report into the initiative in October 2015, warned that it was failing to encourage involvement in the EU legislative process. 'To my knowledge, there have been fifty-one initiatives launched, but not a single one has attained its goal: legislative action. I have talked to many people in civil society who say this whole thing is useless, because the Commission will simply not accept any initiatives,' he said.

The Commission has been very legal, rather than political. I don't think they understand that this is a way of involving people. It takes a lot of time to get a million signatures, but it means that there are a million people that get involved in some way. Every time they reject an initiative which has collected a million signatures, it creates a million eurosceptics.

The European Citizens' Initiative was placed under review by the European Commission to try to make it more user friendly. It remains to be seen whether this form of direct democracy can do anything at all to improve the popular legitimacy of the institutions in Brussels and Strasbourg. It seems like a tiny sticking plaster on the very real sense of detachment felt by many voters between themselves and the EU.

DIPLOMACY AND BRITAIN'S PLACE IN THE WORLD

IN Britain uses its influence in the EU to try and make it more competitive, while foreign policy goals can be enhanced through the collective strength of the twenty-eight member nations in trade talks or other 'soft power' actions such as aid or sanctions on rogue regimes and the response to crises and natural disasters.

OUT Britain can develop new global allegiances through its trans-Atlantic and Commonwealth links, build on its close military cooperation with France and remain a key member of NATO and many other international bodies such as the G8 and G20. It can take its own seat on the World Trade Organization.

KEY STATS The UK has the second highest number of Nobel Prize winners, is the world's fifth biggest military spender, the fifth largest importer, has the fifth highest GDP and is one of five permanent members of the United Nations Security Council.

Vladimir Putin's spokesman touched a raw British nerve when he was quoted declaring that, 'Britain is just a small island ... no one pays any attention to them apart from the Russian oligarchs who have bought up Chelsea.' The taunt at the G20 summit in St Petersburg followed David Cameron's call for military intervention in Syria over its use of chemical weapons – even though the House of Commons had voted against involvement. Putin, the Russian President, was also opposed. Not surprisingly, the reported Russian remark triggered British tabloid outrage and a robust response from the Prime Minister. 'Britain may be a small island, but I would challenge anyone to find a country with a prouder history, a bigger heart or greater resilience,' Cameron said.

> Britain is an island that has helped to clear the European continent of fascism... Britain is an island that helped to abolish slavery, that has invented most of the things worth inventing, including every sport currently played around the world. We are very proud of everything we do as a small island – a small island that has the sixth largest economy, the fourth best funded military, some of the most effective diplomats, the proudest history, one of the best records for art and literature and contribution to philosophy and world civilisation.

Later, at his press conference, Cameron added an important footnote. 'Our music delights and amuses millions, The Beatles, Elgar and ... One Direction have conquered the world.' It was certainly a proud record compared to most countries, including Russia – best known for giving the world Communism, vodka and oligarchs – and which has yet to produce anything in pop music to better The Beatles. Or even One Direction. Moscow officially denied the 'small island' comment, which was allegedly made in a private briefing for Russian journalists. But the controversy came at a sensitive time, with Britain's place in the front rank of world affairs seemingly vulnerable to the rise of developing nations as well as belt-tightening at the Foreign Office and Armed Forces – the full-time British Army head count is being reduced from 102,000 in 2010 to 82,000 in 2020. The minimum number of Royal Navy frigates and destroyers thought to be necessary to assure national security in 1998 was thirty-two, was reduced to twenty-five in 2004 amid cost savings and has fallen to nineteen today.[9] MPs on the Foreign Affairs Select Committee warned in January 2014 that the Foreign Office was 'being stretched, almost to the limit' and 'may be in danger of trying to do too much at a time when capacity is being limited' with targets for a 10 per cent cut in UK-based staff. At the same time as all these cutbacks, the EU has been developing its own overseas representation and presence on the global stage through the European External Action Service created in the Lisbon Treaty of 2009. In December 2013, it had 1,498 staff in Brussels and 1,869 more in 139 delegation offices around the world, while its 2016 draft budget was €633,628,000.[10]

A couple of former Prime Ministers were among the prominent British and foreign leaders and diplomats who were prompted by Cameron's pledge of an EU referendum to come out and warn that Britain's 'position in the world' would suffer by voting to leave. Sir John Major said that 'it would be folly beyond belief, in a world of seven billion people who are binding more closely together, for brave little Blighty to decide she is suddenly going to ... cut off Europe in a thick fog and decide to go on her own.' Tony Blair said:

When people say it is debatable whether leaving would mean that Britain had less influence in the world, it really isn't. Anyone who has held the office of Prime Minister knows that our position within the EU is absolutely central to our position in the world. The idea that we would form equal relationships with China and India with an identity separate from the EU is risible to anyone who has seen how big power politics works. On areas such as trade, EU membership gives us huge commercial advantages. And in the political arenas like the G8 and G20, Britain has far greater heft because we are alongside other EU nations.

Blair knows more than most about the world stage. He ensured that Britain stayed close to the US despite tensions with fellow Europeans – but his decision to go to war in Iraq in 2003 split the EU down the middle and led Gerhard Schroeder, the German Chancellor, to despair that Europe could ever have a meaningful common foreign policy.

Even Cameron, who had criticised several aspects of the EU, was absolutely clear that Britain's place in the world was enhanced by membership. 'We would have to think carefully too about the impact on our influence at the top table of international affairs,' he said in his Bloomberg speech.

There is no doubt that we are more powerful in Washington, in Beijing, in Delhi because we are a powerful player in the European Union. That matters for

British jobs and British security. It matters to our ability to get things done in the world. It matters to the United States and other friends around the world, which is why many tell us very clearly that they want Britain to remain in the EU. We should think very carefully before giving that position up.

It was a clear sign that Cameron believed Britain should stay in.

As one of the few EU members which considers itself an active player on the stage of world diplomacy, Britain has been able to harness EU structures to extend its own foreign policy goals, notably through the added clout of joint sanctions against regimes like those in Iran and Zimbabwe. Rogue leaders like Robert Mugabe and his entourage are stung far more by the loss of travel and banking rights or weapons embargoes in twenty-eight countries than in one. That is why Lord Wright of Richmond, Head of the Diplomatic Service from 1986 to 1991, said that 'it has sometimes been argued that British diplomacy boxes above our weight. Surely, departure from the EU would deprive us of the major ring in which to box?' Another of the country's foremost foreign affairs commentators, Robin Niblett, director of the Chatham House think tank, declared that Britain had an important role to play in the EU in

liberalising the single market, reforming the EU budget, promoting a more interconnected EU energy market, striking trade agreements with increasingly assertive emerging powers, and implementing powerful EU sanctions regimes against countries such as Syria and Iran. The idea that a British government can deliver a better future for its citizens sitting outside these areas of EU decision-making than it can inside is fanciful.

Two former ambassadors to Washington, both appointed by Blair, joined the chorus of leading diplomatic figures concerned with the potential loss of influence in the so-called special relationship with the US if Britain left the EU.

Sir David Manning, Blair's former foreign policy advisor and ambassador to Washington from 2003 to 2007, claimed that America looked to the EU as its 'natural partner' and believed that Britain's role was enhanced as a member. 'Outside the EU, our influence in Europe would be sharply diminished – but so it would be in the United States. The risk to the UK of leaving the European Union is of a rapid drift into international irrelevance,' he said.

Compelling economic arguments are made for the UK's membership of the European Union, not least the importance of the single market in which we do almost half our trade. But equally compelling are the strategic, security and diplomatic interests served by UK membership, interests that would be seriously jeopardised were we to leave the EU.

Manning's successor in Washington, Sir Nigel Sheinwald, who was formerly ambassador to the EU, gave his own warning about the impact of Brexit on Britain's foreign and defence policy:

> On foreign and defence issues, we can exert greater traction globally for our positions when they are backed by the rest of the EU. That's why William Hague, a long-standing critic of the EU's internal processes, nevertheless sees the importance of EU-wide agreement when something needs to be done, for example, on Syria, Egypt, Zimbabwe or Burma.

Support for British membership of the EU came from the very top of the US government. Joe Biden, the vice-president, told *The Times*: 'We believe the United Kingdom is stronger as a result of its membership. And we believe the EU is stronger with the UK's involvement. That's our view.' President Obama himself also weighed in, declaring in a White House statement that 'the United States values a strong UK in a strong European Union, which makes critical contributions to peace, prosperity, and security in Europe and around the world'. But this was not the unanimous view of American politicians. Marco Rubio, a Republican senator for Florida and a candidate for the party's presidential nominee, called the special relationship between Britain and the US 'unshakable' whatever happened in an EU referendum. 'As for Britain's role in Europe, that should be a matter for the British people to decide and for your American partners to respect whatever decision you make,' he said. 'Our alliance, our partnership and our affection for your nation will continue

regardless of the road you choose.' Jeb Bush, the former
Florida governor and fellow Republican candidate, has
said that he would push for a new trade deal between
the UK and the US if the UK voted to leave Europe.
Ted Cruz, the Texas senator and another Republican
presidental candidate, said that a post-EU trade deal
between the UK and the US 'would be an opportunity
to mutually deregulate our economies …Deregulation
is a powerful, liberating economic force that can lead to
significant economic growth – something Lady Thatcher
understood all too well.' They were echoing a strand of
Republican thinking that led the Speaker of the House of
Representatives, Newt Gingrich, to state in 1998 that, 'If,
as appears likely, there is a movement in the US Congress,
as there has been in the Parliament of Canada, to offer
Britain some associate status in the North America Free
Trade Agreement, I would support it.' This was simply
not possible while Britain remained a member of the EU
because the power to conduct trade negotiations is one
that all EU member states hand over to the bureaucrats
in Brussels. Whether or not Gingrich was aware of that,
the American reaction showed a tendency for the US to
split on party lines over the necessity for Britain to stay
in the EU, mirroring the position in the UK itself. John
Bolton, a staunch Republican who was US Ambassador
to the United Nations under President George W. Bush,
wrote that:

> The State Department should remember that Thomas
> Jefferson, its first Secretary, once wrote: 'It cannot be to

our interest that all Europe should be reduced to a single monarchy.' … Until America once again has a president prepared to deal effectively with global threats to US interests, there is obviously little that those of us in opposition can do to support a United Kingdom determined to preserve some measure of democratic sovereignty. But rest assured, you are far better off making up your own minds than having Barack Obama make them up for you.

European leaders want Britain to stay in the EU because of the extra strength this gives to the organisation on the world stage – as well as the extra cash from Britain's net contribution and its strong liberalising influence around the table. José Manuel Barroso went further and warned that the UK's own prestige would suffer if it left. 'From a European perspective, I find it a little bit ironic that some people are suggesting for Britain a role comparable to that of, say, Norway or Switzerland,' he said.

'The fact that some are suggesting for Britain a role that is smaller than the one Britain already has today seems to me a little bit curious.' Barroso said that when David Cameron met President Obama, he had 'much stronger leverage because everybody knows that Britain is a country that is very influential in the shaping of Europe'. While British politicians avoided criticising Obama and Biden for their interventions, they readily attacked Barroso. Martin Callanan, former leader of the European Conservative MEPs in the European Parliament, said:

It is precisely because Britain is such an internationalist country that it does not wish to become just another state in a federal Europe. Britain has its own ties and relationships with the rest of the world. Barroso has become so blinkered about his European project that the idea of a large country standing on its own two feet eludes him. Britain can have a much looser relationship with the EU and still extend its influence in the world. When Cameron visits Washington, he does so as the leader of the USA's most reliable partner and longest-standing international ally, not as just another EU leader.

Nor should Barroso simply be allowed to trash the global influence of Norway, which for a country of just five million maintains a formidable humanitarian reputation, taking a leading role in peace and reconciliation talks in the Middle East (leading to the Oslo Accords), Colombia, Haiti, the Philippines, Somalia, Sri Lanka and Uganda. Switzerland is the location for numerous world bodies such as the Red Cross, World Trade Organization, UN High Commissioner for Refugees and World Economic Forum, and it played host to the 2014 Syrian peace talks.

Cameron has made a strong case for continued EU membership alongside Britain's participation in a number of international forums. In so doing, he highlighted the number of different stages on which Britain plays out its global role.

We are playing our part to build a world that is more stable and more ordered, because it is right in itself and because it is in our own enlightened national interest. Another key part of that effort is our place in international organisations. At the UN. The Commonwealth. NATO. The WTO. The G8. The G20. And, yes, the EU. Membership of these organisations is not national vanity – it is in our national interest.

Strangely he included the World Trade Organization among the bodies where the UK wields influence, even though belonging to the EU denies Britain its own seat at the table – an oversight immediately spotted by the UK Independence Party. 'It is hard to tell if the Prime Minister is being ignorant or dishonest when he claims that Britain is at the top table at the WTO. We are not,' said Nigel Farage, the UKIP leader.

We are represented only through the EU and its trade commissioner. Only if we left the EU could Britain be a true member of the WTO. Independence would mean greater, not lesser influence on the world stage. Likewise, Mr Cameron knows that Britain's membership in the Commonwealth, the G8, the G20 and NATO would be completely unaffected by leaving the EU. He also knows that our permanent membership of the UN Security Council is actually threatened by our continued membership of the EU, which wants a larger role for itself at the UN.

An independent Britain would indeed claim its own seat at the WTO alongside the other 162 members, the size of the body making this more of a symbolic sign of freedom from the EU. Farage was right, however, to raise concerns about the long-term status of Britain's seat on the UN Security Council, where since the end of the Second World War it has been one of five permanent members alongside China, France, Russia and the United States. This is clearly a major source of the UK's international prestige and – whatever one thinks of the UN's effectiveness – places Britain firmly in the first rank of nations globally. A recurring theme of reform plans for the permanent membership is not only to bring in a country from Africa, South America and possibly also India, but also to consolidate the European representation as an EU seat. There would be less logic behind this if Britain left the EU and therefore also its Common Foreign and Security Policy (CFSP) run by its European External Action Service. And despite Blair's assertion that 'anyone who has held the office of Prime Minister knows that our position within the EU is absolutely central to our position in the world', we learned in 2013 that this did not apply to everyone who occupied No. 10. There was one Prime Minister who concluded that Britain would be better off out of the EU – and it was the Prime Minister credited with enhancing the country's global position through cementing a close relationship with the US and acting decisively with military force when circumstances demanded. Margaret Thatcher came to believe that

Britain should quit the EU, according to her biographer Charles Moore.

> Andrew Neil interviewed me about my biography of Margaret Thatcher. He asked me if, after leaving office, Lady Thatcher had come to the view that Britain should leave the European Union. I said yes (I think it happened after the Maastricht Treaty in 1992), although advisers had persuaded her that she should not say this in public since it would have allowed her opponents to drive her to the fringes of public life.

Times have changed considerably since voicing a desire to quit the EU was felt to be beyond the pale in polite society, however, with even the Chancellor of the Exchequer George Osborne and other Conservative Cabinet ministers stating openly that Britain could leave unless the EU was reformed.

The revelation about Thatcher showed that opinion is divided over whether Britain needs to remain in the EU to project itself on the world stage. It is divided between British Prime Ministers and between senior American politicians. But the divide is split on party lines and the weight of opinion is in favour of EU membership. The overwhelming majority of senior diplomats, who perhaps have much to lose through Brexit, believe Britain should stay in the Brussels club to try and make it work better and also to use it to enhance the country's well-established global presence. In the future, economic 'soft power' such as sanctions, trade and development aid will be the key to successful international diplomacy as much as the 'hard power' of military might. The constant struggle to remain relevant and influential in a rapidly changing world was shown by an editorial in China's nationalistic *Global Times* tabloid, which welcomed Cameron on a visit to the capital in 2013 by writing that: 'The UK is not a big power in the eyes of the Chinese. It is just an old European country apt for travel and study.' Britain does still command widespread respect through its impressive achievements as listed by Cameron in response to the earlier Russian jibe but, if it did leave the EU, it would need to work harder to maintain its clout in Beijing and Moscow, not to mention Washington and Brussels.

IMMIGRATION

IN Free movement of workers between the twenty-eight EU countries is one of the four core principles of the Single Market along
with the free movement of capital, goods and services. Any EU
citizen can come to Britain with their family to work, use schools
and the NHS and receive welfare benefits, if they pass an habitual
residence test; Britons are able to enjoy the same rights in other EU
countries.

OUT Britain could regain the right to turn away EU citizens at its
border and could bring in an Australian-style immigration system, only
allowing long-term access to those with shortage skills, like nurses, or
seasonal workers on temporary visas. In this case, UK citizens might
face reciprocal difficulties living and working in EU countries.

KEY STATS 8.28 million foreign-born people including 3.03 million
EU-born citizens live in the UK of whom 853,000 are Polish;[11]
2.2 million Britons live in other EU countries including a million in
Spain.[12] Polling shows that 77 per cent of Britons want fewer immigrants and 56 per cent want the number to be 'a lot' lower.[13] In 2015,
immigration became the most commonly mentioned concern in the
Ipsos-MORI Issue Index, ahead of the NHS and the economy.

One devastating image brought home the dangers
faced by thousands of Syrians fleeing their country's civil war – the sight of three-year-old Alan Kurdi
lying face down on a Turkish beach after drowning on
the treacherous crossing to Greece. The little boy, from
an ethnic Kurdish family, was killed along with his
brother and mother when their flimsy boat capsized.

They were among 805 migrant deaths recorded in the eastern Mediterranean during 2015. The heartbreaking photographs added to pressure on European leaders to provide more assistance to those seeking to escape from Syria. This came at the start of September, just as a bottleneck of asylum-seekers was building up in Budapest when the government there tightened asylum policy, and after a summer that had already seen record arrivals in western Europe of people from north Africa, the Balkans, the Middle East and Afghanistan.

The pictures may have influenced Angela Merkel's humanitarian decision a few days later to allow the crowds from Hungary free passage into her country while sending out a message that all Syrians making it to Germany would be allowed to stay. A record 104,460 migrants had already arrived in Germany during August, drawn by its generous approach to asylum-seekers, but so many were coming that it was no longer possible to carry out proper identity checks before letting them in. After Mrs Merkel's powerful gesture of welcome, a further 409,000 migrants came between 5 September and 15 October. By the end of the year, a total of almost 1.1 million arrivals had been recorded in Germany.

The EU's Schengen system of open internal borders began to break down, with several countries, including Germany, rushing to introduce temporary controls. The influx put a tremendous strain on communities across Germany and caused bitter disputes between EU nations as Mrs Merkel and several other leaders proposed a new method of distributing asylum-seekers around all the

EU nations, to be combined with large holding camps in external border regions. 'We need a binding agreement on the distribution of refugees according to fair criteria between member states,' she told the Bundestag. It was not just a 'challenge at national level, but for the EU as a whole', she added. 'If Europe fails in this refugee crisis, it betrays its founding principles.'

Despite Mrs Merkel's attempt to make the common reception of asylum-seekers a test of EU credentials, several nations including Hungary and Slovakia objected strongly. They were promptly outvoted in a majority decision to impose quotas, which caused an acrimonious split between richer northern and western European nations and poorer eastern countries. Without the goodwill of all nations, the quota system proved impossible to enforce. Britain, which has the ability to opt out of EU asylum and immigration law dating back to the 1997 Amsterdam Treaty, exercised its right not to take part in the scheme. In the same treaty the UK also kept out of the Schengen system, which abolished internal border checks between twenty-six European countries, and which allowed vast numbers of migrants to wander around the continent once they succeeded in crossing an external frontier, until urgent temporary controls were brought in. Seen from across the English Channel, the migrant crisis looked like a failure of EU coordination and security on an epic scale and was seized upon by campaigners for Brexit. In a response to speeches from Angela Merkel and François Hollande to the European Parliament in October 2015 appealing for a common

EU approach, Nigel Farage, the UKIP leader, told the German Chancellor:

> In what must count as the worst piece of public policy seen in modern Europe for half a century, when you compounded the already failing and flawed EU common asylum policy by saying to the whole world 'Please come to Europe' and we saw, frankly, virtually a stampede, and we learnt that 80 per cent of those coming are not Syrian refugees ... what you have done is opened the door to young male economic migrants, many of whom I have to say behave in a rather aggressive manner, quite the opposite from what you would expect to see from any refugee. Yet when that failure is met by objections from countries like Hungary, their opinions are crushed. There is, I think, a bright star on the horizon. It is called the British referendum. And given that none of you want to concede Britain the ability to take back control of our own borders, a Brexit now looks more likely than at any point in modern time.

There were howls of derision for Farage's speech from some Members of the European Parliament. But his words proved prescient in the light of events less than three months later in Cologne. A large mob of men of north African or Middle Eastern appearance were responsible for hundreds of sexual assaults on women during New Year's Eve celebrations, a scene repeated on a smaller scale in several other German cities. It also became clear that several of the Islamic State terrorists who staged the attacks on Paris in November 2015 that killed 130 people had travelled unnoticed among the migrant throng from the Middle East. Just when David Cameron was preparing to make security a central campaigning point for staying in the EU, the failures of its external border controls highlighted deep flaws in its ability to keep its own citizens safe. The impact was shown in a Survation poll in January 2016 which found that 34 per cent of British voters felt more likely to vote to leave the EU because of the Paris attacks, 38 per cent because of the German sexual assaults and 47 per cent because of the Syrian migrant crisis.

There was to be more bad news for Britain as a result of the migration crisis – a review of the Dublin Regulation, the system for returning asylum-seekers to the country through which they first entered the EU, which the UK decided to opt into. This served Britain well, as a country usually reached by migrants after first crossing several other member nations, with the UK share of EU asylum-seekers falling from 12 per cent in 2009 to 3.5 per cent. But it totally broke down in 2015 with many states unable or unwilling to send people back to the first EU country they reached – usually Greece or Italy – and the European Commission proposed a new system that would effectively allocate asylum-seekers to member states on a proportional basis. Even if Britain exercised its right not to opt in, the previous system of sending asylum-seekers back to the first point of entry seemed likely to be scrapped.

The goal of regaining control over Britain's borders in order to manage immigration much better is one of

the key rallying cries of the campaign to leave the EU.
Yet Britain did not experience anything like the same
direct impact of the 2015 migrant crisis as the Schengen
countries because it has a tougher regime than the
other EU nations – it kept out of the zone and retained
passport checks at its borders. The added barrier of the
English Channel makes illegal entry much harder than
for those nations which share land borders. The most
noticeable immediate impact of the crisis for Britain
was that numbers of migrants camped on France's north
coast near Calais and the Channel Tunnel doubled to
6,000 during the summer of 2015, while Eurotunnel cut
freight trains by a third in July to September because
of the security risks posed by migrants trying to reach
the UK. Some of those made it into Britain illegally by
hiding in freight lorries or, in the case of one Sudanese
man, walking the entire 31-mile length of the Channel
Tunnel (he was granted asylum). But how long before
the million-plus migrants of 2015 could legitimately
come to Britain? A study by the Migration Observatory
at Oxford University in 2013 found that 141,000 people
– 7 per cent of those who had come to the UK under
EU rules since 2001 – were born outside the continent.
Somalis were one of the biggest groups, with an estimated 20,000 coming to the UK from the Netherlands
alone, consisting of between one third and a half of the
entire Dutch Somali community.

The Somali case led a caller to LBC Radio in January
2016 to ask Nigel Farage about the migrant men responsible for the Cologne attacks. The UKIP leader replied:

> Those scenes that we have seen in Cologne of those aggressive young males behaving as badly as they were … they will all, if they wish, be coming to Britain in a few short years because after a period of three years, maybe four, they will be able to get German passports, and a German passport is an EU passport, which is a British passport.

He was mistaken, however, because it takes eight years of legal residence to qualify for a German passport, together with a proven knowledge of the German language, adequate means of support and a clean criminal record. Germany has a longer qualifying period than many other EU national passports – in the Netherlands, for example, the minimum period of continuous residence to apply for a passport is five years.

The fate of the deal allowing UK border guards to check vehicles for stowaways at some French ports became the subject of an intense row after David Cameron claimed in February 2016 that Paris could tear up the agreement in the event of a Brexit. That could mean migrant camps like the notorious 'Jungle' in Calais appearing in southern England, the Prime Minister warned. Yet the deal was based on the bilateral Le Touquet Treaty of 2003 and not a part of EU law, causing eurosceptics to accuse him of scaremongering. Lord Blunkett, who signed the deal, backed Cameron. But the arguments in favour of the status quo remain persuasive – not least the French desire not to make its ports more attractive to asylum-seekers trying to reach the UK.

The core argument over EU immigration stems from the 'four freedoms' that form the cornerstone of the Single Market – the free circulation of goods, services, capital and people. The free movement of people means that citizens from EU countries can come to Britain visa-free for a visit of three months, for six months if they are seeking a job with a realistic prospect of finding one, and for an unlimited period to work or study, or if they are self-employed or self-sufficient. They could apply to become a permanent resident after five years. Clearly, the rules make it impossible for a country to impose a limit on the numbers of arrivals, as David Cameron found out after becoming Prime Minister, when he declared that he wanted to cut net inward migration to below 100,000 people a year. Figures in November 2015 put net migration into Britain at a record 336,000 in the year to June, with a net increase of 42,000 in EU citizens on the previous twelve months to 180,000. The net number from countries outside the EU was also up, by 36,000 to 201,000, showing the difficulty in reducing migration flows even from countries where restrictions are not prohibited by EU treaty obligations.

One important thing that has changed enormously since Britain joined the six original EEC members in 1973 is the dramatic enlargement of the EU to include countries with much poorer economies than Britain's. Free movement made perfect sense when all the member countries had broadly comparable living standards and earning expectations. But UK GDP per capita is three times what it is in Bulgaria, Romania and Croatia, the most recent countries to join the EU with a combined population of 33 million, bringing membership to twenty-eight nations and 504 million people. Such was the British government's enthusiasm for new members that Labour ministers regarded it as almost rude to suggest that they should make use of the ability under EU enlargement treaties to impose temporary restrictions for up to seven years on migration from the eight former Communist countries that joined in 2004. 'It is important that we send as positive a signal as possible – not just as a government, but as a whole Parliament – to all the acceding countries,' Beverley Hughes, then Immigration Minister, told the House of Commons in June 2003 while making the case against limiting arrivals from the new member states including Poland, Hungary and the Czech Republic. It would make them 'second-class citizens', she added. 'It is our position that the government should extend to these countries the hand of friendship.' This completely ignored the fact that Britain used temporary restrictions for six years to control migrants from the previous accessions of Greece, Portugal and Spain. It also overlooked the fact that Germany and Austria kept controls on workers from Eastern Europe for the full seven years allowed under EU rules, without suffering a loss of friendship with Poland or their other neighbours.

The Home Office had commissioned independent research from University College London that predicted the number of permanent migrants from the ten new countries would be between 5,000 and 13,000 a year. In fairness, the authors warned that there would be more if other countries had safeguards, which they did, while Britain had none. But it was still dramatically wrong. An average of 170,000 long-term migrants – those staying more than twelve months – came every year from 2004 to 2011. As Labour began to distance itself from the high immigration years of its time in office, Jack Straw, who was Foreign Secretary at the time the new EU countries joined, admitted in November 2013 that failing to apply transitional restrictions on Eastern European migrants was a 'spectacular mistake'. Writing in the *Lancashire Telegraph*, he added that 'net migration reached close to a quarter of a million at its peak in 2010. Lots of red faces, mine included.'

When Romania and Bulgaria joined the EU in 2007, the shock of the 2004 enlargement was so great that Britain imposed restrictions on their citizens for the full seven years. Nevertheless, there was still a large influx from those two countries when free movement began to apply at the start of 2014. Romanians were the third biggest national group coming to the UK in the year to September 2015, behind Indians and Chinese. There were 165,000 registrations for National Insurance numbers by Romanians, the highest national total of the 655,000 EU applications, followed by 122,000 from Polish nationals and 60,000 from Italians. Despite suspicions that a number of people come from poorer countries to take advantage of Britain's welfare payments, as well as the free National Health Service, a European Commission study in 2013 said there was 'little evidence' that so-called benefit tourism motivated

Eastern Europeans to move to countries with more generous benefits.

Healthcare and benefits costs associated with new arrivals from the former Communist countries remained 'very low', it concluded – despite estimating that the additional burden on the NHS was between €1.1 billion and €1.8 billion in 2011 alone. That amounted to 1.1 per cent of health expenditure in Britain. But the report suggested that the economic contribution of the migrants far exceeded these social costs. That was because only 30 per cent of EU migrants in Britain were 'economically inactive' – defined as students, pensioners, job-seekers or home-makers – compared with 43 per cent of the wider British population. Moreover, the government has had an habitual residence test since 1994, strengthened in 2004 with a 'right to reside' test, to weed out benefit claimants with no ties to the UK. Nevertheless, Theresa May, the Home Secretary, insisted that some European migrants abused the EU's free movement laws to become an 'unacceptable burden' as so-called benefit tourists. Despite repeated requests for evidence from the European Commission, May's department offered no figures to back up her claims. 'Finland, Sweden, Germany or the UK did not comment on this matter due to lack of evidence,' the authors of the migrant study noted. There were individual cases of fraud, such as that of Lavinia Olmazu, who helped 172 Romanians illegally claim £2.9 million in benefits after becoming a campaigner for the rights of Roma and was jailed for two years and three months. But it was hard for the Home Office to compete more generally on facts because it simply did not collect data on which European nationalities abused welfare benefits.

The Department for Work and Pensions did compile a report on working-age benefit claims by different nationalities. From an analysis of National Insurance numbers, it found that 5.76 million people were claiming working age benefits in 2011 in Britain, of whom 371,100 were non-UK nationals (6.4 per cent). Of these, 91,310 were from EU countries (1.6 per cent of claimants) including 28,740 from the twelve mainly Eastern European countries that joined after 2004 (0.5 per cent of all benefit claimants in the UK). There were more benefit claimants from Africa (97,760) and from Asia and the Middle East (125,690) than from the entire EU. Country by country, the table of foreign benefit claimants was headed by those born in Pakistan (33,060), then Somalia (25,480) with India in third place (19,380). There were six EU nations in the top twenty countries of UK benefit claimants, led by Ireland in fourth place (15,630) and followed by Poland in seventh place (13,940 or 0.24 per cent of all claimants). These figures suggested that few EU citizens could be 'benefit tourists'. They showed that Europe was the source of less than one third of foreign benefit claimants in Britain. In December 2013, following the media outcry over the lifting of work restrictions on Bulgarians and Romanians, the government added more questions to the habitual residence test and announced that EU migrants would not be able to claim Jobseeker's Allowance until they had been resident for three months. New claims would be limited in most cases to six months' duration.

In response to a Parliamentary Question seeking up-to-date evidence of EU benefit tourism, Lord Freud, the Welfare Minister, said in January 2016:

> The benefits system is one of a range of factors attracting migrants to Britain ... EU nationals are a significant contributor to recent increases. Meanwhile, an analysis of administrative data held by the Department for Work and Pensions showed that between 37 per cent and 45 per cent of all recent EU migrants were in households supported by the benefits system as of March 2013. The government has already introduced tough new measures to ensure that EU jobseekers will have no access to means-tested benefits whatsoever as Universal Credit is rolled out. And now we want to ensure that the welfare system plays no part in the migration decisions of any EU national. The Prime Minister is therefore pursuing further reforms to ensure that EU migrants who come to the UK for low-paid work cannot claim in-work benefits until they have lived here and contributed to our country for a minimum of four years.

The figures quoted by Lord Freud were dismissed as 'very dubious' by Jonathan Portes, of the National Institute of Economic and Social Research, who said that they showed the government had no data on benefit tourism. Lord Freud's answer 'doesn't show any connection at all between people coming here and wanting to claim benefits', Portes said. 'I know lots of people in Whitehall and there's no senior policymaker in Whitehall that thinks benefit tourism is a big problem, or that changing the rules will stop people coming to Britain. I think the government know that and that's why they're trying to blow smoke.' In December 2015, Sir Stephen Nickell, an economist from the Government's Office for Budget Responsibility, told MPs on the Treasury Select Committee that Cameron's proposed changes to the rules on benefits were 'unlikely to have a huge impact' on the number of EU migrants coming to this country. Vote Leave, one of the campaign groups, published analysis suggesting that the National Living Wage starting in April 2016 would be a bigger draw to Britain than the welfare system. The group said it would increase the take-home income of the lowest-earning EU benefits claimants with no dependents by £57.99 per week, or £3,015.48 a year, by 2020.

Nevertheless, Cameron made a four-year ban on claiming in-work benefits one of the key demands of his renegotiation ahead of the referendum. In his Chatham House speech of November 2015, he set out his case, saying:

We now know that, at any one time, around 40 per cent of all recent European Economic Area migrants are supported by the UK benefits system, with each family claiming on average around £6,000 a year of in-work benefits alone and over 10,000 recently arrived families claiming over £10,000 a year. We need to restore a sense of fairness, and reduce this pull factor subsidised by the taxpayer. So I promised four actions at the election. Two have already been achieved. EU migrants will not be able to claim Universal Credit while looking for work. And if those coming from the EU haven't found work within six months, they can be required to leave. But we need to go further to reduce the numbers coming here. So we have proposed that people coming to Britain from the EU must live here and contribute for four years before they qualify for in-work benefits or social housing. And that we should end the practice of sending child benefit overseas. I understand how difficult some of these welfare issues are for other member states. And I am open to different ways of dealing with this issue. But we do need to secure arrangements that deliver on the objective set out in the Conservative Party manifesto to control migration from the European Union.

The results of Cameron's renegotiation, outlined in a draft deal in early February 2016, fell short of his two main welfare goals. He was only able to secure a so-called 'emergency brake' to prevent new EU migrants gaining access to in-work benefits for a limited time once Britain could prove its social support systems were under extreme strain. Even then, the migrants would only be banned from benefits initially and would gradually gain more access to them over the four-year period the longer the worked. Child benefit would continue to be paid to children abroad but cut to reflect the level of benefit in the home country.

There was a more positive outcome for Cameron's

aim of ending abuse of migration rules through sham marriages, with agreement in the draft deal to over-rule European Court of Justice rulings allowing illegal non-EU immigrants to gain residency in Britain after marrying EU nationals.

An independent Britain, after leaving the EU, could impose strict immigration rules like Australia, which only allows long-term access to students, family members and those with skills required in the country. Campaigners for Britain to leave the EU, such as the Conservative MEP David Campbell Bannerman, have argued that the UK could then do bilateral deals for visa-free access with those European economies of a similar size like France and Italy. The problems would start if the EU closed ranks against the UK and insisted on an 'all or nothing' approach to the Schengen zone of twenty-six countries which have abolished internal passport controls. While this does not yet include Bulgaria and Romania, it does cover poorer countries like Poland and Greece. If an independent Britain failed to establish a visa-free arrangement with Spain, for example, home to a million British citizens, then retiring to the Costas could become much more bureaucratic. Spain might not be well disposed to forming good bilateral relations with Britain if it left the EU, or could perhaps use the issue as a bargaining chip over the future sovereignty of Gibraltar. Non-EU migrants to Spain have to fill out much more paperwork, for example criminal record checks and certificates of tax status, while they also have to take the Spanish driving test if they want to own a car, unlike EU citizens whose driving licence is mutually recognised.

If the UK was to leave but then follow non-member Norway into the European Economic Area in order to stay in the Single Market, the government would still be duty bound to follow the market's four freedoms including the freedom of movement of workers. Even Switzerland, which lies outside the Single Market but inside the Schengen travel zone, found it necessary to reach a bilateral agreement with the EU in 2002 to accept the free movement of workers, in exchange for travel and work rights for its own citizens – although Swiss voters narrowly called for quotas of migrants to be restored in a referendum in February 2014.

Opposition to immigration is often fuelled by claims that it drives down wages and deprives British workers of jobs. Yet the Organisation for Economic Cooperation and Development has concluded that a direct link between immigration and the loss of jobs among the host population is hard to prove over the long term.

> An increase in the share of immigrants in the labour force increases unemployment of natives, but this impact is temporary and vanishes between four and nine years after the shock. Beyond this transitory period, the level of the share of immigrants in the labour force does not influence significantly natives' unemployment.

That is the dry economic conclusion but the wider social and cultural impact of immigration means that many voters will make it their top priority in the referendum on EU membership.

To the academic evidence that immigrants boost the country's economy because they tend to be younger and more industrious than the native population, UKIP also has an answer. In a BBC interview in January 2014, Nigel Farage explained his party's policy of a five-year ban on permanent settlement combined with work permits to meet skills shortages:

> If you said to me, 'Would you want to see over the next ten years a further five million people come into Britain and if that happened we would all be slightly richer?', I would say, 'Actually, do you know what? I would rather we weren't slightly richer and I would rather we had communities that felt more united and I would rather have a situation where young unemployed British people had a realistic chance of getting a job.' So, yes, I do think the social side of this matters more than pure market economics.

He would seem to be in tune with voters, with an opinion poll for the BBC by NatCen Social Research finding that 77 per cent wanted fewer immigrants and 56 per cent wanted the number to be 'a lot' lower. Of those who saw immigration as good for the economy, 54 per cent said that they still wanted lower numbers of new arrivals. The question is, how much economic pain is palatable in order to assert tighter control over Britain's borders? With the government officially sticking by its goal to cut annual net migration to below 100,000 a year by 2020, even the Treasury used a net figure of 140,000 a year for annual forecasts in the Chancellor's 2015 Autumn Statement. And its own Office for Budget Responsibility has warned that, with fewer workers coming from abroad, the national debt would be much higher (and by implication so would the need for higher tax or the pressure to cut spending). Immigration will be one of the key topics in the EU referendum and, despite the hotly disputed argument over how much of a 'pull factor' welfare benefits really are, it is the British economy and way of life that are the main draws for EU migrants, most of whom come to Britain to work. The EU's fundamental rules allowing freedom of movement will not change. This means that the only way to regain as much control over who comes to the UK from the EU as the government already has over people from non-EU countries is to walk away from the European club.

INVESTMENT

IN The UK is the EU's top destination for Foreign Direct Investment (FDI), with a market share of just over 20 per cent in 2014, as well as the highest amounts from Australia, Canada, India, Japan and the US.[15] Britain acts as a gateway for investors to the Single Market of 504 million people.

OUT Britain has a range of attractions to persuade international firms to invest such as its flexible and well-educated labour force, quality of life and language advantages, good technology and transport infrastructure, stable and proven domestic legal and political framework, and comparatively low company taxes.

KEY STATS Britain attracted $72 billion in foreign investment in 2014, the highest in Europe and ninth in the world, according to the UN World Investment Report.[16] The UK won 1,988 major investment projects in 2014–15, up 12 per cent year on year, according to UK Trade & Investment.[17] Around half of FDI comes from other EU countries. The UK-based car industry received at least £2.6 billion of foreign investment in 2013.[18]

Nearly 10,000 new cars roll off the Nissan production line in Sunderland every week. By the time it began producing its top-end Infiniti Q30 model in December 2015 following an extra investment of £250 million, the company's plant in the north east had been the biggest car manufacturer in the UK for seventeen consecutive years. Nissan's total investment of £3.6 billion has directly created 6,700 British jobs and a further 27,000 in supply chains. Its success and expansion has encouraged French components maker Valeo, American car seat supplier Tacle and Japanese exhaust and dashboard maker Calsonic Kansei to come to Britain and set up their own factories. Three-quarters of the cars made in Sunderland are exported, with 57 per cent of the 500,238 vehicles made in 2014 going to Europe, 27 per cent staying in the UK, 3 per cent going to Russia and Ukraine and 13 per cent delivered further afield. While the decline of manufacturing is frequently lamented in Britain, the recovery of mass car production, albeit under foreign ownership, has been an outstanding success story in recent years. Foreign Direct Investment (FDI) has revived the (German-owned) Mini as well as (German-owned) Bentley, (Indian-owned) Jaguar Land Rover and (German-owned) Rolls-Royce. The vehicle industry now accounts for 10 per cent of UK exports worth more than £30 billion a year. So it was an important moment when Carlos Ghosn, the chief executive of Nissan, joined the debate about Britain's future with the EU. 'If anything has to change we [would] need to reconsider our strategy and our investments for the future,' he told the BBC at the launch of the firm's Qashqai model in 2012. 'It is a completely different situation if the UK is not part of Europe.' The following year he told an interviewer: 'From the foreign investor point of view I hope that the UK will remain as an EU member.' Ghosn's warnings went to the heart of fears that an exit from the EU would wreck investment in what remains of Britain's manufacturing industry, especially a sector like cars which is so dependent on export sales and component imports.

Eurosceptics were quick to point out that Ghosn had cried wolf before. 'A decade ago, it was not only Nissan but Ghosn himself making remarkably similar imprecise warnings which served to muddy the waters of debate about Europe,' said Global Vision, a eurosceptic campaign group for a basic trade-based relationship with the EU.

Without actually threatening to close the company's Sunderland plant, Ghosn in 2002 warned a UK decision not to join the euro 'might' lead to a reassessment of where to build the next generation of Almera cars. In the end, Britain didn't join the euro and the new Almera was still produced in Sunderland, along with a number of other Nissan models. More than ten years later, business is booming at the plant. Shortly before David Cameron's long-anticipated landmark speech on Europe, Nissan announced a £250 million investment into its UK production facility alongside the creation of 280 new jobs. So should we really be worrying that the ambivalent musings of a company and its boss about our political future with the EU will see them pull the plug on UK production?

But Ghosn was not alone among car-makers in warning about the dangers of withdrawing from the EU. Dave Hodgetts, UK managing director of another Japanese firm, Honda, which has invested at least £1.4 billion in its Swindon plant, said: 'We have very strong markets in Europe, and globally as well, but we are more dependent

on the European region for the exporting of our products. Anything that weakens our ability to trade with
the region would be detrimental to UK manufacturing.'
Stephen Odell, chief executive of Ford in Europe, said:
'All countries should have their sovereignty, but don't
discuss leaving a trading partner where 50 per cent of
your exports go. That would be devastating for the UK
economy.' And Ian Robertson, a BMW board member
and global head of sales, said: 'The UK not only has to
be part of Europe. It has to be a fundamentally active
part of Europe. The thought of a UK outside of Europe
with different trade agreements – sorry, it's not the
way forward.'

While the car-makers made their concerns very clear,
the departure of Britain from the EU would not mean
an automatic crash in automobile production. As Dave
Hodgetts of Honda said: 'It depends on what's negotiated. There would have to be a penalty to being outside
rather than inside – that's the risk I think.' The car
companies are pleading for the stability of the status
quo in dealing with the EU. Will there be penalties for
ending EU membership that would wreck the car industry and dissuade further investment? Campaigners for
withdrawal argue that there need not be any detrimental
impact of Brexit on the success of UK-based car manufacturers. They believe that free trade in goods would
continue between Britain and the twenty-seven remaining EU member states because of a mutual desire to avoid
huge losses on both sides (discussed more fully in the
Trade chapter). To illustrate the folly of failing to agree

a Free Trade Agreement (FTA) on merchandise between an independent Britain and the EU, the eurosceptic Ian Milne, in his paper on The British Car Market and Industry for the Civitas think tank, imagined a telephone call from the German Chancellor to the CEO of BMW.

Good morning Herr Reithofer. I have some bad news for you, and for your employees. Now that the UK is outside the EU, and there's no UK-EU FTA in place, despite the British offer to scrap duties altogether, the EU and therefore Germany will charge 10 per cent customs duty on car imports from the UK, and the UK will charge 10 per cent customs duty on UK car imports from the EU and therefore from Germany. So, from tomorrow, all of your exports from Bavaria to the UK (130,000 high-end BMWs in 2011) will be 10 per cent more expensive, no doubt giving Jaguar cars produced in England quite a lift. Oh, and just to make your day, all those high-margin Minis you produce in Oxford for export to the EU (156,000 in 2011) will also have to bear the 10 per cent EU duty, making them significantly less competitive in Germany, France and elsewhere in the EU. As for your Rolls-Royces, even wealthy EU buyers might jib at paying the upwards of £10,000 extra that the 10 per cent duty will cause. Sorry about the triple whammy, but that's EU politics for you ... Tschüss!

Milne is right that it is very unlikely that the car industry will be hit with tariffs in a trade war following a British departure from the EU, especially given the German surplus of car sales to the UK (Germany exported 474,000 more cars to the UK in 2011 than it imported from Britain). But even a small amount of uncertainty surrounding the smooth continuance of the free trade in goods between Britain and the EU could affect long-term investment decisions.

This nervousness was shown by the official response of the Japanese government to the Government's Review of the Balance of Competences between the UK and the EU in July 2013:

> More than 1,300 Japanese companies have invested in the UK, as part of the Single Market of the EU, and have created 130,000 jobs, more than anywhere else in Europe. This fact demonstrates that the advantage of the UK as a gateway to the European market has attracted Japanese investment. The government of Japan expects the UK to maintain this favourable role.

One of those Japanese companies is Hitachi Rail Europe, which has built several new depots around the country and an £82 million factory to make train carriages in Newton Aycliffe in the north east. Alistair Dormer, the chief executive, echoed the Japanese government line that it had chosen Britain to be its 'gateway' to the EU markets. 'Clearly, we would be concerned as a business if there were any trade barriers or any barriers to doing business in Europe,' he said. Investors wanted Britain to have warm and stable relations with Europe, he added. 'Europe is potentially our biggest market and we would not want anything to happen that would create any barriers or damage the relationship.' He backed calls for structural reforms to the EU, but added: 'My personal advice is we should stay in.' It was not just investors from Japan who were nervous. Juergen Maier, managing director of Siemens UK, the German engineering giant which employs 13,000 in Britain, told a *Sunday Times* debate on business and the EU that leaving Europe would be 'disastrous' for British manufacturers.

It's tough enough as it is to convince my board in Germany to invest in the UK for manufacturing. I'm in competition with other European countries, I'm in competition with China. If we were not within the EU, Siemens would make it quite difficult for me to continue to invest in those factories.

Businesses crave stability in the countries they invest in, as reflected in the main factors cited by decision-makers in the annual UK Attractiveness Survey by EY, a professional services company. In its 2015 report on foreign direct investment, it stated:

The four aspects of the UK that foreign-based companies consider most attractive from an investment location perspective show little change from previous years. They are: the UK's 'quality of life, diversity, culture and language' with 90 per cent rating this criterion as 'very' or 'fairly' attractive [unchanged from 2014]; the 'stability of the social climate' [86 per cent, down from

87 per cent]; 'technology and telecommunications infra-structure' [85 per cent, down from 87 per cent]; and 'education in trade and academic disciplines' [85 per cent, unchanged]. The fifth most important attribute is a new one that we introduced to the research this year – 'access to the European market', which 83 per cent regard as 'very' or 'fairly' attractive. This is given added significance by the prospect of a referendum on the UK's membership of the EU.

The survey also found that investor sentiment towards Western Europe had strengthened in 2015 as problems developed in emerging markets, with 50 per cent of investors regarding it as among the most attractive regions of the world, up from 45 per cent in 2014. North America was the second most favoured region, while China and Russia both suffered big falls in confidence, with India and Brazil treading water.

Uncertainty over Britain's membership could impact foreign investment in the short term, EY also found. Asked if the possibility of the UK leaving the EU would affect investment plans up until the end of 2017, one in eight respondents said they would reduce investment and one in five said they would put it on hold until the situation became clearer. A majority (54 per cent) said it would have no impact while one in ten said they would increase investment.

Investors were also asked how the UK's attractive-ness as a place to invest would be affected if it voted to leave the EU and retained access to the Single Market on similar terms as before, only with no political links to Brussels. The findings revealed very mixed opinions. While 43 per cent said that this scenario would not change the UK's attractiveness, 31 per cent said it would make the UK less attractive, and 22 per cent thought Britain would become more attractive.

Britain retained its lead over Germany in attracting the highest number of investment projects in Europe, the 2015 report from EY said, although the Germans continued to attract more investment from China.

For pro-EU campaigners, the success of Germany in attracting investment, in exporting and in manufacturing is proof that EU membership is no handicap to success in these fields. 'There's a German question for the eurosceptics. Why is China choosing a country that is locked into the heart of what they see as a moribund union?' wrote the europhile former *Financial Times* editor Richard Lambert in 2013. The answer, provided by EY, is that Germany excels in sectors in especial demand in the developing world, such as manufacturing, engineering and chemicals. 'Our European survey data suggests that many investors view the UK as being in a different market from Germany for foreign investment, as a result of the two countries' differing economic and market characteristics,' it said.

The UK is primarily seen as Europe's leader in the provision of services rather than traditional manufacturing, raw materials or chemicals. As discussed further in the chapters on Trade and also The City and Finance, this makes Britain vulnerable to a failure to negotiate continued full access for its services to the Single

Market if it votes to leave the EU, a problem faced by non-EU member Switzerland. However, Mark Gregory, the EY chief economist, speaking several months after David Cameron's Bloomberg speech, said that international companies generally believed that, whatever happened in a vote, Britain and the EU would reach a pragmatic arrangement in terms of trade. Jaguar Land Rover's launch of a new £500 million engine plant in Wolverhampton in February 2014 with a promise to employ 1,400 workers suggested that the company's Indian owners had few qualms. UK corporation tax is set to reduce to 18 per cent in 2020 (it was 30 per cent in 2008), making it the lowest in the G7 group of wealthiest developed nations, compared to the German rate of 29.65 per cent and France's 33.33 per cent. This will go a long way to smoothing over concerns at a fluctuating exchange rate, one of the drawbacks for the UK internationally of not joining the euro, as well as providing a useful hard cash counterweight to less tangible fears about the future outside of the EU.

In October 2015, Jeff Immelt, chairman and chief executive of GE, the giant US corporation that employs 17,000 people in Britain, said that the UK was an 'export country' and that 'good relationships around the world' were more important than its place in the EU. 'As a global investor, it really doesn't matter. We have a big presence here and we're a big exporter from here. So it's important that the UK has good relationships around the world, but I don't really think that its place in the European Union makes that much difference.'

Almost half of investors surveyed for the government's trade body UK Trade & Investment in 2010 said that a factor in their decision to plough money into the British economy was the ability to serve the European market from a base in an English-speaking country. But it was not given as the most important factor in their decision, with 90 per cent of respondents saying that their top motivation was servicing the UK market. Being close to customers and being able to access centres of expertise were also among the reasons given. The Business, Innovation and Skills Department has concluded that 'surveys suggest that access to the Single Market is not the sole reason for choosing the UK as a destination for investment. Being a global hub, having a good established business network, the English language and good international linkages were all cited as factors.' A House of Commons Library report in September 2013 on the Economic Impact of EU Membership on the UK concluded:

On the whole, it is reasonable to conclude that member-ship of the Single Market is one of a number of important determinants of FDI... On the one hand, the removal of barriers to trade eliminates an important incentive to physically locate abroad, meaning the Single Market could be argued to discourage intra-EU investment. On the other, membership of the Single Market should stimulate inward investment in the UK from outside the EU, since by doing so, they can access twenty-seven other EU markets tariff-free.

Maintaining this tariff-free access to the rest of the EU was the fundamental reason for the appeals from UK-based car companies, Hitachi Rail and the Japanese government itself to keep the status quo in trade relations with the EU from the perspective of international investors. Back in 2000, research on the jobs linked to EU membership by the National Institute for Economic and Social Research (NIESR) warned that a breakdown in trade relations could mean a drop of one third in foreign investment in manufacturing and one tenth in services. The challenge for British negotiators in the event of Brexit – if they want to preserve current high levels of foreign investment – is to keep the open border trading relationship with European neighbours. Otherwise there could be a sizeable reduction in foreign firms willing to put money into the British economy, and that would worsen living standards.

Brexit could still bring some benefits for investors, the House of Commons report added.

Outside the EU, the UK may be able to establish a regulatory regime more favourable to overseas investors that could offset the effect of its departure. In particular, the UK would regain competence to negotiate international agreements on Foreign Direct Investment with other countries, something which it has not been able to do since the Lisbon Treaty entered force in 2009.

JOBS

IN Pro-EU politicians regularly argue that at least 3 million jobs depend on Britain's EU membership, implying that these would be at risk if the UK left.

OUT If Britain does a deal to remain in the EU's Single Market, like non-EU member Norway, or negotiates a Free Trade Agreement to retain full trading access, then many of the supposed job losses will be avoided. Jobs lost by leaving the EU would eventually be replaced as trade expands elsewhere.

KEY STATS South Bank University in 2000 said that 3.45 million UK jobs were related to trade with the EU; the National Institute of Economic and Social Research in 2000 put the figure at 3.2 million jobs. With 29.4 million employed in the UK in 2012, these reports suggest that more than one in ten jobs are related to the EU.

Business for Britain was created in 2013 to campaign for a significant return of EU powers under David Cameron's policy of renegotiating the UK's relationship before holding the referendum on membership. To add weight to its goal of a dramatically slimmed-down deal with Brussels, the eurosceptic organisation commissioned extensive polling that showed businesses believed the costs of the Single Market outweighed the benefits. Not mentioned in a 26-page report issued by Business for Britain on its polling results, however, was another finding that showed 6 per cent of firms (sixty-two out of 1,024) surveyed said they would be forced to close down in the UK if voters decided to leave the EU. Based on turnover, half of these were small businesses, 32 per cent medium-sized and 18 per cent large. The overlooked finding was discovered in the small print of the research and highlighted by British Influence, another group created in response to Cameron's referendum plan. British Influence is a pro-European group formed to campaign for the positive engagement of the UK in the EU. It quickly realised that talk of business closures and therefore job losses could help its argument for staying in the EU and its Single Market. It scaled up the forecasts based on 1,024 responses to all businesses in the UK and concluded that 1.5 million jobs were at risk. 'Tucked away amidst all these interesting results is a bombshell,' wrote Peter Wilding of British Influence on the ConservativeHome website in November 2013.

On page sixteen of the poll is the conclusion that over 50,000 businesses would close if the UK left Europe – putting 1.5 million jobs at high-risk. Those 5 per cent of small businesses, 8 per cent of medium-sized ones and 9 per cent of large ones, which said they would close, equates to 1,501,040 jobs – according to figures worked out by British Influence with the help of a professional statistician. The Department for Business, Innovation and Skills works this out at around 50,000 small, 2,500 medium and 500 large companies at risk of closure. Worse still, these figures for business closures and job losses could also more than double, since 7 per cent of all businesses surveyed would be 'unsure' about their future if Britain left the EU after a referendum.

Not only was this a taste of the arguments to come during the EU referendum campaign, but it was also the first time in nearly thirteen years that a clear figure had been put on direct job losses from Brexit. Before this, politicians continued to use figures from 2000, when two pieces of academic research concluded that either 3.45 million or 3.2 million UK jobs were related to trade with the EU. The 1.5 million estimate was less than half of this amount but the first based on extensive polling data. It was also more concretely related to jobs that would actually be lost in the event of British departure. As Peter Wilding pointed out: 'People we are supposed to support are saying: if we leave, we will close and jobs will go.'

It was about time that the figure of more than 3 million potential job losses was laid to rest. No politician was more fond of repeating the claim than Nick Clegg, the former Deputy Prime Minister, who used it to suggest that leaving the EU will jeopardise that number of jobs. In August 2013, Clegg told the *Newcastle Journal* that

there are up to 3.5 million jobs either directly or indirectly linked to our membership of the world's biggest single market, and yet, because of political dogma, UKIP and the Conservatives want to put that at risk. Yes, the EU needs to reform, but people should remember this is about people's jobs, their monthly pay packet, and they shouldn't play around with that.

The pro-EU Labour MP Keith Vaz has also used the figure, telling the *Sunday Mirror* in January 2013 that 'over half of trade and 3.5 million jobs in Britain are dependent on the EU'. Gordon Brown challenged the then opposition leader David Cameron at Prime Minister's Question Time in 2008, saying, 'Why won't you wake up to the fact that 3.5 million jobs are dependent on our membership of the EU?' But even the authors of the original studies do not believe that 3.5 million jobs will be lost if Britain were to leave the EU.

The figure originates from two pieces of research commissioned in 2000 by another, long defunct, pressure group called Britain in Europe, which campaigned for Britain to join the euro. In one study, the European Institute at South Bank University said that exports to the EU generated direct employment of 2.53 million jobs in British industry and supply chains, while the secondary impact of spending on British goods and services arising from revenue generated by exporting to the EU supported 'indirect employment effects' amounting to a further 917,000 jobs. The report said that:

> The aim of the present investigation is not an overall evaluation of EU membership, but rather an estimate of the employment effects that result from the exports of goods and services from the UK to the EU. Although many previous studies have sought to answer the question of what would have happened if Britain were not a member of the EU, we do not seek to test this counterfactual hypothesis.

The researchers used export figures from 1997, when trade with the EU (then fourteen member states) made up 55.8 per cent of British goods exports (it had fallen to 50.5 per cent in 2014 for twenty-six member states[19]) and 34.4 per cent of British services exports (it was 36.7 per cent in 2014[20]). A key variable in the researchers' calculations (the import component of exports) was taken from 1990, which was the best available figure at the time. The data is now long out of date.

The second study was by the National Institute for Economic and Social Research (NIESR) in London which calculated that about 2.7 million British jobs were directly related to goods and services sold to the EU, while a further 500,000 were supported by other sources of demand for firms which derive much of their activity from exporting to Europe. That made 3.2 million jobs linked to trade with the EU. The report added:

> As the experience of the 1960s indicates, there is no reason why being outside the EU should necessarily involve mass unemployment, although living standards would probably be slightly lower ... exports to the rest of the EU would not fall to zero if the UK were to leave the EU.

The report concluded that living standards would be affected by EU withdrawal, with gross national income declining after twenty years by 1.5 per cent and output by 2 per cent. As mentioned in the previous chapter, it warned that Foreign Direct Investment in manufacturing in Britain could drop by a third and in services by 10 per cent if Britain pulled out of the EU. As for job losses in the event of British withdrawal from Brussels, around 175,000 would be lost after three years, but these would be reabsorbed at lower wage levels in the longer term, the report estimated. 'There is no *a priori* reason to suppose that many of these [jobs], if any, would be lost permanently if Britain were to leave the EU,' it concluded. So, according to research commissioned in 2000 by the pro-euro Britain in Europe, there would be similar levels of jobs whether the UK was in or out of the EU, although they would probably be paid at a slightly lower level. In a statement at the time, as the figures began to be used as a political football, Martin Weale, then director of the NIESR, said: 'Although a large number of jobs are now connected to EU exports and the income they generate, it is not the case that many of these would be lost permanently if Britain was to leave the EU.' One of the authors of the South Bank research, Professor Iain Begg, said in 2011 that he would not expect mass redundancies if Britain withdrew from the EU, on the assumption that there would be some kind of deal to continue with trade, even if the UK was no longer involved in setting the rules in Brussels. And Jonathan Portes, the current director of the NIESR, tweeted in September 2013 that the research was 'past [its] sell-by date'. In an article, he called the claim that up to three million jobs would be jeopardised by a British departure one of the great red herrings of the EU debate.

Even if the potential negative impact on trade and invest-ment ... were actually to materialise, such claims are totally implausible, and certainly not based on evidence. Over the medium to long run, the main determinant of employment and unemployment is the supply side of the economy – the flexibility of the labour market and the skills and qualifications of potential workers – so there is unlikely to be any significant long-run impact. Trade makes us richer and more productive – so a reduction in trade may well feed through to a reduction in real wages – but most conventional economic models do not suggest that it creates (or destroys) substantial numbers of jobs over the medium term.

Full Fact, the independent fact-checking organisation, has twice issued warnings to politicians about their continued use of the 'more than three million jobs' scare over EU withdrawal. In its first review in November 2011, it said that

> any statistics based purely on trade with the EU do not offer a fair cost-benefit analysis of the impact of EU membership on the labour market, since the two are not necessarily directly correlated. Free trade agreements between the EU and non-EU countries exist for some ten countries in Europe and others elsewhere, including a Free Trade Agreement made with Switzerland in 1972. A figure which depends entirely on UK exports with the EU does not necessarily show that UK withdrawal from the EU would dramatically alter this trade in a negative way.

In its second review in July 2013, it added:

The point is that the three million figure doesn't tell us anything about the number of jobs linked to British membership of the EU as an institution, only about those linked to the EU as an export market. What would happen to that market in the event of a British exit is a matter of speculation. This is no small distinction to make and, with a referendum in the horizon, it's only fair that the public are supplied with the correct information to inform their vote. Unfortunately certain politicians have made a habit of conflating the two, with Danny Alexander [former Liberal Democrat Chief Secretary to the Treasury] following in the footsteps of Nick Clegg and Ed Balls [former Labour shadow Chancellor] on this matter. We are concerned this number has acquired a life of its own and are therefore writing to those concerned to ask that greater care is used in the future to avoid misunderstanding about this figure.

That leaves the figure of 1.5 million job losses based on Business for Britain polling in 2013 and extrapolated by British Influence. This is a warning of how bad things could get if there is a catastrophic breakdown of trading relations between the EU and Britain after a vote to leave. It would not necessarily apply if the UK were able to stay in the Single Market like Norway or negotiate a Free Trade Agreement to have full access for those companies that continued to meet EU standards and rules even though Britain has withdrawn from political involvement. As discussed in the previous chapter over the car industry, there is every incentive for Germany in particular and the EU in general to continue to keep close trading links with Britain in the event of its withdrawal from the EU. Around one million jobs in Germany, 500,000 jobs in France and 300,000 jobs in Italy are said to be linked to exporting to the UK. Some eurosceptics claim that Brexit will bring a domestic jobs boom. The Bruges Group, a think tank opposed to European integration, has argued that a million jobs would be created in Britain by leaving the EU but staying in the European Economic Area, like Norway, because of the effective tax cut for businesses freed from 70 per cent of the EU's rules and regulations.[21] As discussed in other chapters, particularly on the City and Investment, some sectors will go through a turbulent readjustment period and probably see jobs lost in the UK if the relationship with the EU changes. But the level of job losses depends on a 'known unknown' – the exact status of the new relationship between Brussels and the UK. If a post-Brexit Britain can only achieve the same level of access as Switzerland, which has free trade in goods but not completely in services, the financial sector is likely to see thousands of jobs disappear as international banks, finance and insurance companies move staff into the EU. There are also areas where new jobs could be created, including opportunities arising from trade deals between Britain and other countries which are not possible while the EU retains full control of international trading policy, and job-creating freedoms for smaller companies released from European social and employment regulations.

PEACE AND HUMAN RIGHTS

IN The European Union was awarded the 2012 Nobel Peace Prize for advancing the causes of peace, reconciliation, democracy and human rights in Europe. The EU has provided the political and economic framework for peace among nations that went to war with each other regularly for centuries and bound together France and Germany which fought three times in seventy years.

OUT Britain would continue to be a key member of NATO which is also responsible for binding European nations together and guaranteeing the peace since the Second World War. Would the UK's departure really fuel a rise in separatism and hostility that eventually results in the disintegration of the EU and war?

KEY STATS More than 50 million lives were lost in the Second World War, making it the deadliest conflict in history, which started just two decades after the First World War claimed more than 10 million lives.

Edward Heath, the man who took Britain into the European Economic Community in 1973, was named after his uncle – a man he never knew because he was among the one million Britons killed in the Great War of 1914–18. As a 21-year-old undergraduate, the future Conservative Prime Minister went on a student exchange trip to Germany in 1937 to see for himself the Nazi regime that came to power in the years of economic depression and would soon plunge Europe into an even more devastating conflict. Heath was introduced to

two of the senior Nazis, Joseph Goebbels and Heinrich
Himmler, and watched in horror as Adolf Hitler gave
one of his trademark ranting speeches at a Nuremberg
rally. The following year Heath experienced conflict in
Europe for the first time when he came under machine-
gun fire on a visit to Spain to meet leaders of the Popular
Front resisting General Franco's forces. Just a few years
later, as a captain in the Royal Artillery, Heath joined
the Normandy landings and the Allied advance across
war-ravaged Europe, taking part in the destruction of
the French cathedral city of Caen and being greeted by
cheering crowds in liberated Antwerp. He saw at first
hand the ruins of German cities like Düsseldorf which
were unrecognisable as the places he had visited just a
few years earlier. 'The centre was nothing but a mass
of rubble. It proved impossible for me to find my way
to the street, let alone the house, where I had stayed as
a student,' he wrote. Promoted to the rank of major,
Heath's unit was put in charge of a prisoner-of-war
camp near Hannover and Heath even commanded a
firing squad that executed a Polish prisoner for rape.
'My generation could not live in the past,' Heath wrote
about his ambition to see Europe united in peace. 'We
had to work for the future. We were surrounded by
destruction, homelessness, hunger and despair. Only by
working together had we any hope of creating a society
which would uphold the true values of European civili-
sation.' The EEC, the forerunner of the European Union,
was created by men like Heath who had experienced the
horrors of two wars initiated by European enemies.

David Cameron declined to attend the Nobel Peace Prize ceremony for the EU in Oslo in December 2012 but paid tribute in his Bloomberg speech to the part played by the European Union in maintaining peace between the continental powers. He acknowledged that today's generation accepted almost unthinkingly that peace was the permanent state of international relations in Europe. 'What Churchill described as the twin marauders of war and tyranny have been almost entirely banished from our continent,' he said.

> Today, hundreds of millions dwell in freedom, from the Baltic to the Adriatic, from the Western Approaches to the Aegean. And while we must never take this for granted, the first purpose of the European Union – to secure peace – has been achieved and we should pay tribute to all those in the EU, alongside NATO, who made that happen. But today the main, over-riding purpose of the European Union is different: not to win peace, but to secure prosperity.

It could be argued that the two fundamental goals, peace and prosperity, go hand in hand, given the role played by the economic crisis of the 1930s in the rise of Nazism. A similar sense of national crisis and exploitation by foreign powers was felt in Greece during the struggle to save the euro, and spawned a menacing far-right movement, Golden Dawn, even as the EU was awarded the Nobel Prize for contributing to 'the advancement of peace and reconciliation, democracy and human rights in Europe'. The award also conveniently overlooked the murderous conflict in the Balkans in the 1990s following the break-up of Yugoslavia when more than 100,000 lost their lives and which the EU was powerless to prevent despite its attempts at diplomacy. In presenting the prize, the official announcement did acknowledge that 'the EU is currently undergoing grave economic difficulties and considerable social unrest' but added that

> the Norwegian Nobel Committee wishes to focus on what it sees as the EU's most important result: the successful struggle for peace and reconciliation and for democracy and human rights. The stabilising part played by the EU has helped to transform most of Europe from a continent of war to a continent of peace.

Although the Nobel award specifically mentioned the EU's work for human rights, it is important to be clear that the EU is a separate organisation to the Council of Europe – the body which oversees the European Court of Human Rights. Popular confusion between the two is understandable. A pan-European human rights body was a brainchild of Winston Churchill, Britain's wartime Prime Minister, at the same time as he also called for a political alliance of European nations. 'We must recreate the European family in a regional structure called, it may be, the United States of Europe,' he said in a landmark speech in Zurich in 1946. 'The first step is to form a Council of Europe.' (Although Churchill was not always clear about Britain's role as an observer or a participant in these European organisations, he also said in Zurich that 'in all this urgent work, France and Germany must take the lead together. Great Britain, the British Commonwealth of Nations, mighty America, and I trust Soviet Russia – for then indeed all would be well – must be the friends and sponsors of the new Europe and must champion its right to live and shine.') Churchill took part in the first sessions of the Council of Europe assembly in 1949 and 1950 when British lawyers helped to draft the European Convention on Human Rights, which was designed to protect citizens from a return to the barbarity of Nazism or the oppression of Communism by guaranteeing – among other things – rights to life, liberty, freedom of expression and a fair trial. All member states of the Council of Europe agree to abide by the Convention and accept judgments on it by the European Court of Human Rights (ECtHR) set up in 1959. Although its judgments are binding on member nations, it has no means of enforcement other than moral authority.

The British government complained that the ECtHR exceeded its mandate to stand up for the oppressed when it ruled that denying prisoners in Britain the right to vote breached their human rights, as did passing 'whole life' sentences with no chance of review. It was also angry at judgments which held up the extradition of radical Islamists Abu Hamza to the US and Abu Qatada to Jordan. 'If Parliament decides that prisoners should not get the vote then I think they damn well shouldn't. It should be a national decision taken by our Parliament,'

David Cameron said in December 2013. Cameron vowed to restrict the court's powers, saying 'we need to clip its wings'. However, the ECtHR's real power over British law comes from British legislation, the Human Rights Act 1998, which gave the Convention legal force in British courts. That is why the Conservatives made a manifesto commitment to repeal the Act and replace it with a British Bill of Rights, although unlike UKIP they have not proposed withdrawing from the jurisdiction of the ECtHR altogether. The Bill of Rights would 'break the formal link between British courts and the European Court of Human Rights, and make our own Supreme Court the ultimate arbiter of human rights matters in the UK'.

The British debate over the ECtHR comes, confusingly, in parallel with the EU deepening its own human rights powers. In recent years the EU has sought to become more of a 'rights body' not only for its own member states and their neighbours but for the globe. In 2007, the EU set up a Fundamental Rights Agency based in Vienna to monitor racism and xenophobia; it also set up an EU Institute for Gender Equality based in Vilnius. The original EEC treaty did not have any reference to human rights but the European Court of Justice first claimed jurisdiction over fundamental rights in 1970. The EU seriously began to encroach upon the role of the Council of Europe in 2000 when it adopted a Charter of Fundamental Rights containing fifty-four rights (the original Convention had eighteen Articles) including the right to strike, to marry and found a family, to collective bargaining and fair working conditions. It was incorporated into EU law in the Lisbon Treaty of 2009, although Britain and Poland secured a protocol to exempt their legal systems from any new rights. In 2013, however, the legal effectiveness of the protocol was called into question, when High Court judge Justice Mostyn called it a 'misleading product of political compromise because on any view the charter enunciated a host of new rights not expressly found in the European Convention on Human Rights'.

In Mostyn's view 'it would seem that the much wider charter of rights is now part of our domestic law' and would remain so, even if the Human Rights Act was repealed. This led Lord Mance, a justice of the UK Supreme Court, to warn that the European Court of Justice was attempting to impose the Charter of Fundamental Rights on British judges. 'Ultimately, the European project must rest on mutual trust, goodwill and cooperation,' he said in a speech to a legal conference in 2013. 'Mutual trust is an article of faith of the European Union. But it requires real sensitivity to build and maintain. Over-ambitious steam-rolling of centralising projects in order to promote the European project can achieve precisely the opposite result.' Sir William Cash, chairman of the House of Commons European Scrutiny Committee, warned in a letter to *The Times* in December 2015 that the EU's Charter of Fundamental Rights 'binds our judiciary and Parliament'. He added: 'The charter has serious implications for the fight against terrorism and for immigration issues. The last Labour government sought to exclude this charter in a protocol. The protocol has failed and the European Court of Justice is now applying it. The European scrutiny committee in the last parliament, having taken extensive evidence from ministers and experts, recommended, in its report, amendment of the European Communities Act 1972 to exclude the applicability of the charter to the UK. It is illogical for Parliament to repeal the Human Rights Act 1998 and yet not to override the Charter of Fundamental Rights.' In January 2016, it was revealed that the government was looking to ensure that the British Bill of Rights would include a declaration that British courts are not bound by the EU Charter of Fundamental Rights.

The development of the EU into a global peace-promoting rights body is being led by the European External Action Service (EEAS) created in the Lisbon Treaty to represent the EU around the world. Under its first head, the Labour peer Baroness Ashton of Upholland, the EEAS created the new post of EU Special Representative (EUSR) for Human Rights in 2012. Stavros Lambrinidis, a former MEP and Foreign Minister of Greece, was chosen to travel the world pressing the case for the downtrodden and campaigning against the death penalty. 'All cooperation as well as trade agreements with third countries contain a clause stipulating that human rights are an essential element in relations between the parties,' the EEAS says on its website.

The European Union views all rights as universal, indivisible and interdependent. It actively promotes and defends them both within its borders and when engaging in relations with non-EU countries. The EU's human rights and democracy policy encompasses civil, political, economic, social and cultural rights ... With a financial support of €1.3 billion between 2014 and 2020, the European Instrument for Democracy and Human Rights supports, inter alia, non-governmental organizations promoting human rights, democracy and the rule of law; abolishing the death penalty; combating torture; and fighting racism and other forms of discrimination; as well as observing elections around the world.

A British withdrawal from the EU would not stop its self-declared mission to spread peace and human rights. In some areas it would lead to a more coherent EU that no longer had to deal with British resistance to closer harmonisation of defence, employment and social affairs, foreign policy, justice and home affairs, migration policy, tax and economic matters to name just the most prominent areas of regular disagreement. But could a British departure have the ultimate effect of tearing apart the EU itself and – as the first serious backwards step since the Treaty of Rome was signed by the first six member states in 1957 – be the beginning of the end of the dream of a united Europe? Some commentators foresee other nations emboldened to quit the EU by a British withdrawal. 'There would be many unintended consequences from a Brexit, of course, depending on how skilfully Britain's exit treaty was drafted,' wrote Hugo Brady of the Centre for European Reform.

If one Union member secedes, that increases the chances of another many times over: Denmark and the Czech Republic might look to the door ... as could, let's say, a newly arrived member state defying Brussels over the rule of law and human rights. So the other members and the institutions are unlikely to make Britain's exit treaty favourable for their own individual reasons and to protect the integrity of the Union. But it is still quite likely that if Britain left, other countries would eventually too.

The enormous sums of money handed to poorer countries to invest in their infrastructure would certainly make newer member states think hard before leaving, making the richer, northern nations the most likely candidates to follow an independent Britain out of the EU. But the loss of Denmark or Sweden would not be terminal to the EU. The organisation fundamentally exists to bind together France and Germany, the two countries at the heart of the terrible conflicts that caused so much destruction in the past two centuries, from Napoleon to Hitler. Although there can be no doubting the sense of crisis if a founder member like the Netherlands quit, only a French or German departure would destroy the EU and threaten the European peace we take for granted. And after Jacques Chirac followed Tony Blair in calling a referendum on the EU Constitution in 2005 only to see it lost, Paris has learned its lesson on putting the EU to a public vote.

PROSPERITY

IN The Single Market has boosted national income through increased trade between European nations. The overall impact of the EU on prosperity is less clear, however, because of the costs of regulation, customs duty on non-EU imports, higher food prices and the disputed impact of EU migrants.

OUT Britain could try to negotiate full access to the Single Market to maintain strong trading and travel links. It would be free to make its own trade deals with non-EU countries and cut duties on imports. Only if it left the Single Market, however, could it also scrap expensive red tape for businesses and control EU immigration more tightly.

KEY STATS The government says the benefit of the Single Market is worth £3,500 per household. The Confederation of British Industry claims that the EU benefits the UK by £62–78 billion a year. In 2015, deductions and receipts from Britain's estimated gross EU membership fee of £17.78 billion left a net contribution of £8.47 billion (for a full breakdown of Britain's EU contributions, rebate and receipts see table on page 248).

At the dawn of the millennium, the EU set out an ambitious ten-year plan to succeed in the new century. The Lisbon Strategy, signed in the Portuguese capital in March 2000 by the then fifteen member nations under the chairmanship of Prime Minister António Guterres, aimed to 'make Europe by 2010 the most competitive and the most dynamic knowledge-based economy in the world capable of sustainable economic growth with more and better jobs and greater social cohesion'. The plan aimed to see 70 per cent of the adult population in work, up from 63.4 per cent in 2000. The ultimate goal was 'to enable the Union to regain the conditions for full employment'. This was to be achieved by a mixture of the economic competitiveness typical of northern European nations and the social support systems championed by France and other southern countries. There were targets to increase training, cut red tape for new company start-ups and fund millions of euros of research projects. 'The Lisbon Strategy is going to bring about a revolution in the way we work,' said Mr Guterres. Fellow centre-left leader Chancellor Gerhard Schroeder of Germany said that 'it shows we are prepared to move away from the old industrial society toward a new, high-technology and communications-based one'. It was, as the *International Herald Tribune* observed, 'a bid to surpass the United States in the Internet age'. It didn't work. There were to be no European rivals to touch the success of Amazon, Apple, eBay, Facebook, Google, Microsoft, Netflix or Twitter. By 2010, the European economy was in the middle of a double-dip recession and unemployment was steadily rising.

To be fair, the failure of the Lisbon Strategy was not entirely Europe's fault. The economy was hit by the financial hurricane which started in the US with the collapse of Lehman Brothers investment bank. But even before then the EU never looked like meeting its targets, with employment peaking at 67.1 per cent in the fifteen member states in 2008 (the addition of ten Eastern European countries in 2004 brought the overall rate down further) and falling to 65.8 per cent by 2010. Portugal itself fared particularly badly, with a recession soon claiming the job of Mr Guterres in 2001 and the euro crisis forcing the country to take drastic reforms that cut the employment rate to 61.8 per cent by 2012. Prosperity was replaced in many EU member states by austerity, with the most devastating effects seen in Greece, where the level of unemployment among those aged under twenty-five reached 60 per cent in January 2013, and Spain, where it hit 56.8 per cent in September 2013.[22] Europe felt more like a continent in decline by the end of the Lisbon Strategy with a level of social payments considered unsupportable by Mr Schroeder's replacement as the German Chancellor, Angela Merkel. 'If Europe today accounts for just over 7 per cent of the world's population, produces around 25 per cent of global GDP and has to finance 50 per cent of global social spending, then it is obvious that it will have to work very hard to maintain its prosperity and way of life,' she said in December 2011.

Outside the straitjacket of the single currency, Britain avoided the worst of the euro crisis. David Cameron maintained in his Bloomberg speech that 'today the main overriding purpose of the European Union is ... to secure prosperity'. But assessing just how important the EU is to the UK's standard of living is notoriously difficult to do and no government has attempted a cost-benefit analysis of membership. There are various claims about the extra wealth generated by the EU's Single Market, which has undeniably increased trade and commerce between the twenty-eight member states and added to Britain's national income. There are also some negative factors to be taken into account on the balance sheet when working out the overall impact of the EU, however. These include the cost of regulations, higher food prices as a result of the Common Agricultural Policy, missed global opportunities as a result of focusing on the European market, more expensive imports from outside the EU thanks to the tariffs and quotas of its Customs Union, and, of course, Britain's membership fee. The bigger picture of prosperity is further complicated by the economic and social impact of intra-EU migration. Put all these together in one giant calculation and some analysts believe that the purely economic impact of membership is negligible. Others have claimed gains of up to 6 per cent of GDP, although how much of this would be permanently lost in the event of leaving the EU is also hotly debated. With so many variables, the outcome of cost-benefit studies often seem to reflect the author's attitude towards the importance of the EU itself.

The starting point of these calculations is the contribution transferred from the Account of Her Majesty's Exchequer held at the Bank of England to the European Commission in twice monthly instalments. The estimated gross total of £17.78 billion in 2015 was reduced by £4.86 billion thanks to Britain's rebate deal to £12.92 billion, or £35.4 million a day. The £350 million a week figure often cited by Brexit campaigners is the gross figure before Britain's rebate is deducted, which reduces it to £248 million a week before the Treasury makes its payments. The UK also received public sector funding of £4.45 billion back from Brussels, leaving a net contribution of £8.47 billion, according to Treasury provisional figures.[23] Around £1.4 billion was also received in the form of grants directly to the private sector, mainly for research, while £328 million was transferred from the UK in overseas aid channelled through the European Development Fund run by the European Commission and additional to the EU budget. The rebate, won by Margaret Thatcher in 1984 after nearly five years of negotiation, has saved a nominal £86.2 billion over thirty-two years. That's £7.4 million a day. In contrast to entire EU spending of €141.3 billion in 2015, the UK government spent £735.5 billion in 2014/15. 'The European Union's budget is modest in size compared to national wealth,' said José Manuel Barroso, announcing agreement on an EU seven-year framework budget of nearly €1 trillion for 2014–20. While this will be roughly 1 per cent of the EU's Gross National Income, it is misleading to compare it to national spending because the EU is a bureaucracy which does not pay for public sector workers such as nurses, teachers, social workers or an army, even if its laws increasingly affect their working lives. The sum total of EU GNI has also increased greatly as the number of member states expanded from nine when Britain joined to twenty-eight, putting unexpected extra cost burdens on net contributors like the UK. The Account of Her Majesty's Exchequer now pays ten times more in real terms to Brussels than it did in 1973.

Britain is consistently the second-largest net funder of EU coffers behind Germany and ahead of Italy and France. Most of the money goes towards subsidising farmers and funding infrastructure and employment projects, especially in poorer regions of Europe. In 2015, the proportion of the EU budget spent on the Common Agricultural Policy was 39.6 per cent, or €56 billion, way out of kilter with its EU average gross value added contribution to the economy of 1.7 per cent – and just 0.62 per cent in the UK. British farmers and landowners receive funding from Brussels under two main headings, direct farm payments and rural development, but the UK's net contribution to the agriculture budget – sometimes portrayed as a subsidy to competitors – amounted to €3.4 million a day. According to an analysis by the OECD, European taxpayers paid €105 billion in 2008 to farmers through subsidies and tariffs, as well as national programmes. Just over half of this came directly from the EU budget. The UK's share of the total was around €8.27 billion, made up of €4.6 billion in farm subsidies through EU and national spending, while British consumers paid a premium for their food of €3.67 billion.[24] With 25.5 million households in the UK, that worked out at €324 each extra per year for agricultural support. If Britain left the EU, it would escape the Common Agricultural Policy but would need to give some funding to its farmers to ensure that they did not lose out to subsidised overseas rivals. It is not just farm products, however, but a range of goods imported from outside the EU that are more expensive because of the

EU's common external tariff, such as footwear with a border tax of up to 17 per cent and most other clothing which is charged 12 per cent to enter the EU. Some of these tariffs could be cut by an independent Britain, as they exist to protect jobs in other EU countries, for example shoe production in Italy. 'Although they [tariffs] raise prices for consumers, they also help producers by shielding them from more price competitive imports,' said a research paper on the economic impact of the EU by the House of Commons Library in September 2013. 'While the government would be free to set its own tariffs outside the EU, removing the protection they afford to certain industries could prove politically difficult, given that the costs will be specific and localised, but the benefits diffuse,' it added.

The difficulty of putting a single number on the economic impact of Britain's EU membership over the years was neatly summed up by a House of Commons Library review of the various attempts:

Many of the costs and benefits are, in certain respects, subjective, diffuse or intangible; and partly because a host of assumptions must be made about the terms on which the UK would depart the EU, and how the government would fill the policy vacuum left in areas where the EU currently has competence. Any estimate of the effects of withdrawal will be highly sensitive to such assumptions, and can thus be embedded with varying degrees of optimism. This perhaps helps to explain why the wide range of estimates from the EU cost-benefit 'literature' can appear influenced by the prior convictions of those conducting the analysis.

Even an evaluation of the Single Market requires layers of complicated economic modelling and many 'heroic assumptions' according to one such study by the Centre for Economic Policy Research (CEPR) in 2008, written by academics from Oxford and Berkeley, California. Its ultimate conclusion was that 'European incomes would have been roughly 5 per cent lower today in the absence of the EU'. The creation of the Common Market and its Customs Union brought about a step change in growth, it said, because politicians could appeal to the spirit of European integration to overcome strong domestic resistance to labour market reforms and the liberalisation of protected sectors. The UK 'almost certainly' suffered substantial losses as a result of the Common Agricultural Policy but, if it had never existed, countries 'would probably have gone on protecting their farmers' anyway, they said. The Single Market achieved fewer gains than the original Common Market, the study argued, because 'the 1980s was a period that saw a good deal of domestic liberalisation and deregulation in Europe, spurred by the examples of Reagan in the United States and Thatcher in the United Kingdom'.

A more specific UK analysis by the Institute of Economic Affairs updated in 2001 concluded that:

Many costs and benefits of EU membership are intangible ... An assessment of those costs and benefits which can be quantified suggests the net effect of withdrawal on the British economy would be small – probably less than 1 per cent of GDP. If a special relationship with the rest of the EU were arranged, there might be a small benefit.

Leaving the Common Agricultural Policy would represent 'a clear gain to Britain' and, while there might be a loss in Foreign Direct Investment, 'fear of adverse economic consequences should not deter a British government from seeking to change the relationship of the UK with the EU, or, in the last resort, from leaving the Union'. According to an Institute of Directors paper in 2000, 'the costs of EU membership outweigh the benefits significantly. Moreover, because of the significance of the CAP, there is a huge discrepancy between those who receive (farmers) and those who give (taxpayers).' The IoD put the cost impact of the Common Agricultural Policy as 1 per cent of GDP and the annual cost to the UK economy of the 'EU social welfare model' at another 1 per cent. Overall, it decided that the net annual cost of EU membership was 1.75 per cent of GDP.

A report by the generally pro-EU National Institute of Economic and Social Research (NIESR) in 2000 came to the opposite conclusion, saying that 'the level of real gross national income would be approximately 1.5 to 1.75 per cent lower outside the EU than inside' with GDP permanently 2.25 percentage points lower. It reviewed investment by US-owned companies in Europe since the mid-1960s and argued 'that membership of the EU ... and hence participation in the Single Market Programme [has] a significant positive impact on the location and scale of investment'. In 2004 the think tank Civitas claimed that the annual direct net cost of EU membership was probably 4 per cent of GDP, made up of £20 billion from regulation, £15 billion from the CAP and £5 billion from the net membership fee. The study claimed that there was 'an absence of any convincing evidence in the UK or elsewhere that the Single Market has actually delivered net benefits for the economies of member states'. However, successive studies for the European Commission claimed a permanent GDP boost of 1 per cent (in 1996) and 1.8 per cent (in 2002), while its 2007 analysis of the Single Market effect from 1992 to 2006 claimed a 2.15 per cent rise in GDP. Competition in government procurement had enabled savings of 10 to 30 per cent, it said. An internal paper for the Department for Business Innovation and Skills (BIS) from 2012 claimed that the European Commission's 2007 study, which gave no figures for individual countries, 'implies that the gain to UK GDP was in the region of £25 billion in 2006'.

In evidence to the House of Lords EU Select Committee in 2011, BIS said that

economic evidence shows that the single market has delivered substantial economic benefits. EU countries trade twice as much with each other as they would do in the absence of the single market programme. Given that, according to the OECD, a 10 percentage point increase in trade exposure is associated with a 4 per cent rise in income per capita, increased trade in Europe since the early 1980s may be responsible for around 6 per cent higher income per capita in the UK.

According to Vince Cable, then BIS Secretary, in a newspaper article in May 2012, this translated to a benefit of £3,500 for each household in the UK. A fellow Lib Dem minister in the same department was more circumspect in a parliamentary answer a few months earlier, however. Ed Davey wrote that

> available estimates show that the greater level of trade liberalisation achieved through the single market leads EU countries to trading currently twice as much with each other as they would do otherwise. As a result, the Single Market may be responsible for income gains in the UK between 2 per cent and 6 per cent, that is, between £1,100 and £3,300 a year per British household.

If ministers in the same pro-EU party and department of government cannot agree on the benefits of the Single Market, it would seem an impossible task to find any figure to command general respect.

At the other end of the spectrum, Patrick Minford, Professor of Applied Economics at Cardiff Business School, a supporter of the Better Off Out campaign to leave the EU, has estimated the cost of the EU to the British economy at between 11.2 per cent and 37.7 per cent of GDP, or £170 billion to £570 billion. Minford attributes the bulk of these costs to EU regulations, which he costs at between 6 and 25 per cent of GDP – a vast range and an upper figure far above other estimates. In 2013, the eurosceptic think tank Open Europe put the cost of the 100 most expensive EU regulations at £27.4 billion a year, equivalent to just under 2 per cent of GDP, adding,

> it would be wrong to assume that these regulatory costs would magically disappear if the UK were to leave the EU. The UK government would probably want to keep a good number of these laws in part or in full – anti-discrimination laws, some health and safety rules, food safety standards, and so forth.

According to official government Impact Assessments, costs were exceeded by benefits. A closer look at these official assessments shows just how they are able to claim economic advantages, however. They strive to find benefits from effects such as a better work/life balance, reduction of accidents and higher productivity. Some of the assumptions made are wildly ambitious – for example the Impact Assessment on the EU's Climate and Energy Package. This stated that the cost would be £20.6 billion and the benefits between £9.2 billion and £242.1 billion. That's quite a range and one that no private sector business would ever tolerate. The explanation for the unfeasible potential economic impact ranging from a £11.4 billion cost to a net benefit of £221.5 billion stated: 'Benefits will depend on other's actions and the emissions concentration trajectory the world is on. High end of range reflects world where EU action is pivotal in achieving a global deal.' This effectively meaningless cost-benefit analysis was signed off by the then responsible minister, former Secretary of State for Energy and Climate Change, Ed Miliband.

Another attempt at placing a value on EU membership was made by the Confederation of British Industry in November 2013. It asserted that:

> It is not unreasonable to infer from a literature review that the net benefit arising from EU membership is somewhere in the region of 4–5 per cent of UK GDP or £62–£78 billion per year – roughly the economies of the North East and Northern Ireland taken together. This suggests that each UK citizen has benefited from EU membership to the tune of around £1,225 every year for the last forty years.

The CBI did not carry out any fresh research to arrive at this figure but analysed five earlier studies, including the CEPR paper from 2008 putting the benefit at 5 per cent of GDP along with others claiming benefits of 2.25 per cent, 2.1 per cent and 2 per cent of GDP, as well as one that claimed a net cost to consumers of 2.5 per cent. The pro-EU CBI's findings were clearly on the higher end of the consensus. Again, it showed the difficulty of reaching a single figure to sum up the EU's impact.

The exercise of attempting a crude cost-benefit analysis is frowned upon in Brussels for missing the point of the intangible benefits of nearly seventy years of peace and progress in Europe. The European Commission UK argued:

> It is far too simplistic and perverse to confine the
> European Union to a price tag. There are an array of
> benefits ... that are difficult to quantify in cash: such as
> being part of a market of 500 million people, a cleaner
> and safer environment, and better security. It's like saying
> that it costs money to buy a house without saying that
> you need a house in the first place and that you would be
> in much worse situation without it!

Britain, of course, could move into a house that is either semi-detached from the EU by emulating Norway, or on its own plot by formally leaving the Single Market. The real question that will face voters in the in/out referendum is what would then be the impact on the national balance sheet. In January 2016, Pimco (Pacific Investment Management Co.), a global investment management firm based in California, predicted the uncertainty alone from a vote to leave would be enough to reduce gross domestic product by as much as 1.5 per cent in the subsequent twelve months and prevent the Bank of England from raising interest rates. Several factors with important economic effects that contribute to a feeling of prosperity – notably jobs, immigration, investment and trade – are discussed in depth in other chapters of this book. But there are undoubtedly powerful arguments that the Single Market with its freedom of movement has positive economic benefits, leading to the position of UKIP's Nigel Farage quoted earlier that he would 'rather we were not slightly richer' in return for the ability to block EU migrants.

The winner of the €100,000 Brexit Prize given by the Institute of Economic Affairs in 2014 for the best paper on managing EU departure also called for Britain to leave the Single Market to escape its onerous laws. The author, Iain Mansfield, admitted that the economic gain from leaving could be negligible. He concluded:

> Administratively, the government will need to strengthen its capacity in a wide range of areas from trade negotiations to anti-trust enforcement. Current levels of funding from the EU to sectors and regions should initially be maintained domestically, including in agriculture, to prevent economic shocks whilst the surplus should be recycled to help pay down the deficit. Measures such as tax breaks and supply-side incentives would help preserve the UK's position as the number one inward investment destination in Europe. The outcome would be to accelerate the shifting pattern of UK's exports and total trade away from the EU to the emerging markets, where the majority of the world's growth is located. A more business-friendly regulatory regime and the new security of the City of London from European interference will enhance competitiveness and compensate for the partial loss of access to European markets. The total long-term impact is estimated to be between -2.6 per cent and +1.1 per cent of GDP, with a best estimate of +0.1 per cent. Although the years immediately surrounding the exit are likely to feature some degree of market uncertainty, if the right measures are taken the UK can be confident of a healthy long-term economic outlook outside the EU.

Rating agency Moody's published a report in December 2015 entitled 'Government of the United Kingdom: EU exit would be negative for UK economy; post-exit policy choices will drive credit impact'. Moody's said:

> If the UK were to leave the EU, the credit impact for the sovereign and the implications for its rating would depend primarily on what new trade arrangements the UK government could achieve, as well as its other economic policy choices. Moody's might assign a negative outlook to the UK's Aa1 rating in the event of a vote to withdraw from the EU, to reflect its view that exit would have negative consequences for the UK economy and hence potentially for the UK's credit strength ... The cost savings on the government's contributions to the EU budget are modest at around 0.6 per cent of GDP per annum and in the rating agency's view UK-based businesses would continue to have to comply with EU regulation even after exit, if they wanted to sell into the Single Market. Moody's also notes that EU regulation has not impeded the UK's flexible labour and product markets, nor does the EU seem to be a key constraining factor for extra EU trade, as e.g. Germany's strong trade links with China and other emerging markets show.

Kathrin Muehlbronner, a senior vice-president at Moody's, added:

> Exit would be negative for trade and investment in the UK, given the close links with the EU as the UK's

single most important trading partner and largest source of foreign direct investment. These negative effects outweigh the benefits from exit such as cost savings for government and a reduced regulatory burden for businesses in our view. The UK could face a potentially prolonged period of uncertainty, which in itself would be damaging to confidence and investment. A Swiss-style series of bilateral agreements or a comprehensive free trade agreement would invariably take time to negotiate and this process wouldn't be easy.

A feeling of prosperity is also about more than the ability of government and the economy to boost GDP. Work/life balance, social mobility, community cohesion, quality of the environment and personal health all contribute beyond the confines of an accountant's balance sheet. The independent think tank, the Legatum Institute, has been compiling an annual World Prosperity League table since 2007 based on eight main factors: economy, opportunity, governance, education, health, security, personal freedom and social capital. Britain was placed fifteenth in 2015, down two places on the previous year, slipping because of poorer outcomes for life expectancy and the healthy years citizens can expect to live compared to other developed countries, as well as lower relative enrolment in tertiary education at university and vocational training. Prosperity was also being held back by bureaucracy and inefficiency in government, the Legatum Institute said. Would the UK rise higher in the table outside the EU? The top two countries in the world according to the

Legatum table on www.prosperity.com were Norway and Switzerland – two European nations outside the EU. The top EU country, third-place Denmark, proved that it was possible to be a member of the continental club and achieve that elusive feeling of prosperity regarded as a key aim of EU membership.

SOLIDARITY AND
REGIONAL SUPPORT

IN Britain was instrumental in creating the EU's regional funding system to raise living standards, improve infrastructure and create jobs in poor European areas. The UK received €1.3 billion in 2015 from the €51.1 billion annual budget for regional spending in the twenty-eight EU countries.

OUT Britain would save its €6.4 billion annual payment towards EU regional funds and could choose how much to spend on UK projects. Non-EU member Norway pays a contribution towards poor eastern EU countries in a deal to smooth access to the Single Market, while Switzerland also makes a payment as part of its agreement with the EU.

KEY STATS Britain will receive €9.57 billion from 2014–20 in EU regional funds, made up of €457 million for Northern Ireland, €795 million for Scotland, €2,145 million for Wales and €6,174 million for England.[25] Britain received €10.6 billion in 2007–13 and paid in €36 billion.

Perched precariously on the top of Europe's tallest coastal cliff, the glass-bottomed viewing platform at Cabo Girão opened in 2012 and was one of the more recent of many EU-funded tourist attractions on the island of Madeira. The price tag for the platform, car park and café came to €2.5 million, made up of €2 million provided by structural funds from Brussels and €500,000 of 'match-funding' from an island which had become addicted to EU cash. Madeira, a tiny outpost of Portugal in the Atlantic Ocean off the coast of Africa with a population of 267,000, has attracted €2 billion in EU regional funds in the past twenty-five years. In the rush to grab the cash, little thought was sometimes given to the practical implications of the building projects. The €29.7 million Lugar de Baixo marina built in 2004 on the west of the island for luxury ocean-going yachts was never used after waves cracked the sea wall, while the accompanying €1.2 million restaurant complex was damaged by rockfall from the cliffs above which tore a hole in the roof.

Portugal has collected more than €60 billion in regional support funding from the EU since it joined in 1986 and went on a construction binge so notorious that it was given its own name, '*a política do betão*' (the politics of concrete), as politicians competed for vote-winning infrastructure projects. In 1989, Portugal had just 130 miles of motorways. Twenty years later, it had 1,777 miles – a lot of motorway in a country barely 300 miles long and 125 miles wide. It now has four times more miles of motorway per inhabitant than Britain and 60 per cent more than Germany. The irony is that, with the government forced to introduce road tolls as a condition of its €78 billion bailout deal following the collapse of the economy in the euro crisis, motorway use plummeted. The journey from Lisbon to Porto cost €22 in tolls, causing many drivers to take the smaller local roads and shun the EU-funded motorway system that was supposed to bring growth and jobs to the country.

The EU's seven-year budget for 2014–20 has earmarked a colossal €367 billion in 2016 prices for regional projects, more than a third of all spending. As part of its agreement to join in 1973, Britain was instrumental in pushing for a system of funding to modernise Europe's poorest regions as a counterweight to the huge sums dished out under the Common Agricultural Policy that mainly supported traditional farming lifestyles. The aim was to make sure that no areas were left behind as cities grew more prosperous thanks to the increasing trade made possible by EU membership and consumed national infrastructure spending. Or, as the Treaty on European Union puts it, to 'work for the sustainable development of Europe based on balanced economic growth and ... promote economic, social and territorial cohesion, and solidarity among Member States'. The amounts of cash distributed by Brussels grew exponentially when the former Iron Curtain countries joined after 2004 but they have not been the biggest beneficiaries – from the beginning of their memberships until 2011, Spain, receiving the most so far, has secured €131.4 billion while Greece was handed €61.7 billion.

Britain's share of EU regional funding has dropped markedly as it became relatively more prosperous compared with the new member states but some regions have benefited significantly over the years. From the passenger terminal at John Lennon Airport to the 11,000-capacity Echo Arena and BT Convention Centre in the former King's Dock, the revitalisation of Liverpool owes much to EU regional funding for Merseyside worth £840 million in 2000–06 and £268 million in the 2007–13 budget period. Under EU rules for regenerating poorer areas in wealthier countries, the money was given on condition that equal sums came from the national authorities or private providers, meaning that the Liverpool Cruise Terminal – a huge floating dock for ocean liners built in the Mersey in 2007 – was paid for with £9 million from the UK government and £8.6 million from the EU's European Regional Development Fund. Liverpool's city centre and docklands have been transformed from the desolation left by the decline of the 1970s. The economic statistics show an improvement, too – Merseyside's GDP in 2012 was 80.2 per cent of the European average, up from 70 per cent in 1994, although the benchmark level dropped when the former Communist countries joined in 2004. Liverpool is a tangible example of the impact of European spending in the UK, even if some of the organisations that benefited were fined by Brussels in 2013 for failing to display the EU logo on their projects. Yet the British government has long argued for a fundamental reform of regional spending, which would have meant Merseyside never receiving a euro from Brussels.

As far back as 2003, Gordon Brown, then Chancellor in the Labour government, argued that only the poorer member countries – those with an economy worth 90 per cent or less of the EU average – should receive regional funds. His logic for this was the philosophy of subsidiarity, the EU term meaning that decisions should be taken at the most relevant level of government, either

European, national or local. 'When the economic and social, as well as the democratic, arguments on structural funds now and for the future so clearly favour subsidiarity in action, there is no better place to start than by bringing regional policy back to Britain,' Brown wrote in *The Times*. The Open Europe eurosceptic think tank calculated that, with a threshold of 90 per cent of GDP for receiving cash from Brussels, Britain would have saved €4.6 billion from its gross contribution of €36 billion for regional funding in the 2007–13 budget period. In 2012, Mats Persson, director of Open Europe, said:

> In terms of an EU policy to target for reform, this is an open goal for Mr Cameron: it will save UK taxpayers billions, return powers from Brussels and allow the UK to run a far more effective domestic regeneration and regional policy, while still committing Britain to providing financial assistance to Europe's poorest regions.

In the face of overwhelming opposition from recipient countries, the Conservative and Liberal Democrat coalition gave up on this reform, however, to concentrate on cutting overall spending levels in the seven-year EU budget period from 2014 to 2020. A quick look at the potential impact from the cut in regional funding showed why reform stood no chance – the two main losers would have been Greece (a loss of €17 billion based on the 2007–13 figures) and Spain (a loss of €21.4 billion), at precisely the time when their own national economies were in dire straits because of the euro crisis and needed every cent of assistance to keep afloat.

David Cameron's decision to abandon any attempt to secure radical changes to regional funding during negotiations on the 2014–20 EU budget was reluctantly accepted by MPs on the Communities and Local Government Select Committee. But they urged the government not to give up on future reform of the main fund, called the European Regional Development Fund (ERDF). 'It is clear that withdrawing funding entirely from wealthier Member States is not supported for the 2014–20 ERDF round and we agree with the government's decision not to pursue it in negotiations,' the committee concluded. 'The government should, however, continue to put forward its arguments with the aim of securing enough support from other Member States for subsequent ERDF rounds.' Alarmingly the committee said that they could find no convincing evidence that the EU's enormous regional funding programmes had delivered demonstrable long-term benefits.

The EU's Structural and Cohesion Funds were set up to try and address some of the fundamental economic and social weaknesses of the least-developed regions of the EU. Although there have been some individual local successes it is difficult to prove that the funds have had a significant impact at a regional level. We looked at Cornwall and the Isles of Scilly, which ... has obtained the highest level of ERDF funding [in the UK] since 1994. This region faces particular problems which partly stem from its geographic position; EU funding will not resolve these issues. It can, however, still play a part in mitigating their effects – for instance through a Superfast Broadband project aimed at boosting productivity by connecting 10,000 businesses. However, as Professor Steve Fothergill [of the Centre for Regional Economic and Social Research at Sheffield Hallam University] told us, 'many of the problems we are dealing with in some of the less prosperous regions are deep-seated, and will take decades to turn round'. Although the majority of benefits are realised in later years, the evidence available to us suggests that ERDF 2007–13 has not yet made a significant impact. It is not even possible to conclude that the 2000–06 ERDF round has done so, because of the lack of robust evidence. The challenges facing regions such as Cornwall and the Isles of Scilly are profound, and ERDF can only provide part of any solution.

The cuts proposed by Gordon Brown and Open Europe, but resisted by almost every other EU nation, were taken up by campaigners from the Fresh Start group of Conservative MPs. In their manifesto for powers that David Cameron should have tried to take back from Brussels to national level as part of his renegotiation of Britain's relationship with the EU before the referendum, they wrote:

Regional Development Policy should be decentralised by limiting EU funds to those member states with GDP per head of less than 90 per cent of the EU average. This would provide more funds to those poorer member states, and end the needless recycling of funds among the wealthier member states. It could also result in a 15 per cent cut in the EU budget and enable wealthier member states to make their own decisions about how to support their own regions.

While this was the clear view of Conservative MPs, it was not shared by some of the UK regions themselves – and strongly opposed by the devolved Welsh government. The region of West Wales and the Valleys was the biggest recipient of regional funding in the 2007 to 2013 period with around €2 billion. Derek Vaughan, a Labour MEP, warned against regional funding for Wales becoming decided in Westminster and 'subjected to the whims of the Tory-Lib Dem government' instead of being allocated by the EU. In 2012, he wrote: 'It is a staggering leap of faith by Open Europe to believe that Wales would continue to receive fair and equal treatment under a coalition that has already shown its lack of commitment to Wales.'

A spokesman for the Welsh Government said:

Our position is clear – European regional policy should not be 'repatriated' to the UK. We are determined to ensure we secure the best possible deal for Wales. Structural funds have helped to mitigate the worst effects of the recession in Wales – helping nearly 41,000 people into work and helping to create 12,000 jobs and 2,450 enterprises – and the new programmes will allow us to build on the progress made to date in creating the environment for jobs and growth, helping to transform our communities and improving opportunities for people across Wales.

Not everyone believes that the EU funding for Wales has been worthwhile, however. Guto Bebb, the Welsh Conservative MP for Aberconwy, has compiled a list of 'white elephant' projects including Canolfan Cywain, a rural heritage centre in north Wales built with £900,000 of EU money plus match-funding. Opened in 2008 with an exhibition space, café and children's playground, it failed to pull in sufficient visitors and closed in 2012. 'The EU has created a series of white elephant projects,' Bebb told the *Sunday Telegraph*. 'These schemes, once built, have either closed or need large amounts of public funding to keep them open.' The EU's Court of Auditors has been very critical of the lack of rigorous controls on regional spending. Its report in July 2013 into the €65 billion spent on road projects in the EU since 2000 concluded that 'insufficient attention was paid to ensuring cost-effectiveness of the projects'. It found that motorways were often being built where regular express roads would have solved the traffic problems at just over half the price. Out of twenty-four road schemes audited, costs overran by 23 per cent on average and construction time overran by an average of nine months. Calculated per 1,000 square metres of road, the lowest average costs were found in Germany of €287,043 while the highest were in Spain at €496,208. 'There is no evidence that this can be explained by labour costs,' the auditors remarked.

While the potential savings for the Treasury and taxpayer are massive from withdrawing from the EU and its regional funding programme, Britain would probably not entirely escape the obligation to fund Europe's poorer areas if it left the EU. If it emulated non-member Norway by joining the European Economic Area (EEA), giving it full access to the Single Market but no decisive say over the rules, Britain would be obliged to contribute to the EEA Grants. These are bilateral gifts from the EEA states (Norway, Iceland and Liechtenstein) to the newest countries of the EU. The amounts are negotiated every five years and are technically voluntary, although the EU expects payments in return for Single Market access. The amount Norway paid shot up tenfold when the first batch of former Communist countries joined the EU in 2004, and by another 25 per cent after Bulgaria and Romania joined in 2007. Norway paid €1.3 billion in 2004–08 and €1.8 billion in 2009–13, putting the non-EU member seventh among the net contributors to EU funding, although still paying much less than if it had actually been a full member.[26] Similarly Switzerland, from its position as a member of the European Free Trade Association (EFTA), agreed to pay 1 billion Swiss francs (around £654 million at 2012 prices) for projects in the ten countries which joined the EU in 2004, adding 181 million Swiss francs for Romania and 76 million Swiss francs for Bulgaria when they joined the EU in 2007.[27] When Croatia joined the EU in July 2013, Switzerland pledged 45 million Swiss francs for bilateral projects 'to strengthen economic and political relations' between the two countries. Various attempts have been made to estimate the amount that Britain would be obliged to pay towards projects in the EU's poorer states in return for continued access to the Single Market or Swiss-style bilateral trading conditions. In 2006, the Swiss government estimated that EEA membership would cost it 32 per cent more, while full EU membership could cost six times as much, after receipts from Brussels, based on a gross contribution increase of 786 per cent. If it can be inferred from this that the UK would pay one-eighth of its overall fee to return to the EFTA relationship used by Switzerland, then the estimated 2015 gross charge of £17.8 billion would be reduced to £2.23 billion, while the price of staying in the Single Market through the EEA would be around £2.9 billion a year.

SOVEREIGNTY

IN Britain shares sovereignty in a range of policy areas with the other twenty-seven EU nations to make decisions together on laws proposed by the European Commission, arguing its case in the European Parliament and Council of Ministers. It retains a veto over tax and defence matters and control over its currency. Parliament must implement EU law and obey rulings of the European Court of Justice.

OUT Parliament would be obliged to follow some EU laws if Britain joins the European Economic Area like Norway. Companies trading in Europe would still have to meet EU legal and technical rules, and comply with its competition policy, none of which the UK would have a say over. Outside the EU but in the EEA, Britain would regain sovereignty over important areas including trade and agriculture policy and VAT.

KEY STATS 6.8 per cent of primary legislation (Statutes) and 14.1 per cent of secondary legislation (Statutory Instruments) implemented EU obligations between 1997 and 2009.[28] The government estimates that around 50 per cent of UK legislation with a significant economic impact originates from EU laws.[29]

For much of the last century, a British traveller's credentials to roam the world were contained in a distinctive hard-backed blue booklet bearing the title 'BRITISH PASSPORT' above the Royal crest on its cover. First introduced in 1920, the blue passport began to be phased out in 1988 and replaced with a smaller burgundy document standardised in size, colour and format with the other EU countries. It bears the title

'EUROPEAN UNION' above 'United Kingdom of Great Britain and Northern Ireland'. The idea of harmonising passports across Europe had been agreed as far back as December 1974 at a meeting of heads of government attended by Harold Wilson, a Labour Prime Minister. The details were finally signed off in June 1981 at a meeting of foreign ministers under a Conservative Prime Minister, Margaret Thatcher. The new European-style booklets removed the word 'British' from in front of the word 'Passport'. It was a tangible sign that British sovereignty was, literally, being erased. The new passports were gradually introduced over the next decade, coincidentally at the same time as the Maastricht Treaty created the notion of EU Citizenship – a status normally reserved for those living in a nation state. It seemed as if the deal Britain agreed in the 1970s to pool sovereignty to facilitate the Common Market was being extended to cover much wider areas of national life, touching on deep questions of identity and control over domestic affairs. This fuelled British fears about continental ambitions to create a United States of Europe, an ambition frequently mentioned at the time by Chancellor Helmut Kohl of Germany – and led to Thatcher's famous warning in her 1988 Bruges speech that 'we have not successfully rolled back the frontiers of the state in Britain only to see them reimposed at a European level, with a European super-state exercising a new dominance from Brussels'.

Clearly the actual British sovereign has not been replaced by the EU, although the institution of monarchy has benefited from various injections of European blood over the centuries from George of Hanover to Prince Albert of Saxe-Coburg and Gotha and Prince Philip of Greece and Denmark. Ultimate sovereignty in the UK, defined as independent legal authority over its territory, traditionally rests with Parliament. The EU changed this. Edward Heath explained that joining its forerunner, the European Economic Community, in 1973 would entail 'a sharing and an enlargement of individual national sovereignties in the general interest' and there was 'no question of any erosion of essential national sovereignty'. He was not so clear on what were to be regarded as 'essential' and non-essential areas. The European Court of Justice had already claimed ultimate jurisdiction over essential national sovereignty in areas of shared powers in a ruling in 1963, declaring that 'the Community constitutes a new legal order of international law for the benefit of which the states have limited their sovereign rights'. Another pro-European politician, the former deputy Labour Party leader Roy Hattersley, criticised Heath for refusing to acknowledge the sacrifices necessary to make Europe work: 'Nothing has more injured the idea of Britain in Europe than Edward Heath's foolish assurance (given at the time of our entry into the Common Market) that membership would involve no loss of sovereignty.' But speaking in 2000, Hattersley admitted that the pro-European case had been built on concealing the real fate of British national sovereignty:

What we did throughout all those years, all the Europeans, was say, let's not risk trying to make fundamental changes by telling the whole truth, let's do it through public relations rather than real proselytising ... spin the argument rather than expose the argument ... Joining the European Community did involve significant loss of sovereignty but by telling the British people that was not involved, I think the rest of the argument was prejudiced for the next twenty or thirty years.

Tony Blair shared Heath's view that sovereignty could be shared and enlarged, and vowed to protect Britain's interests by 'retaining the veto in areas where it is essential' while adding that 'sovereignty has to be deployed for national advantage'. In the view of both Heath and Blair, British sovereignty was not something that belonged under lock and key in Whitehall or Westminster but could be bartered and bargained in pursuit of national goals. Although she did not spell it out at the time, this was also what Thatcher practised when she agreed to sacrifice Britain's right of veto over dozens of policy areas by allowing Qualified Majority Voting (QMV) to facilitate decision-making among ministers from the member states meeting in the European Council. 'We could never have got the Single Market without an extension of majority voting,' Thatcher commented in 1993. Every British Prime Minister from Heath to Gordon Brown handed over more national sovereignty to Brussels, until David Cameron's government legislated in the EU Act of 2011 to hold a referendum on the next transfer of power by a change in the EU treaties. Asked if the British Parliament would be sovereign after his EU renegotiation, Cameron's assertion on BBC1's *The Andrew Marr Show* in January 2016 that 'the British Parliament is sovereign now' was true only in the sense that Parliament has agreed the EU should have legal competence in various fields and the British government remains able to repeal the European Communities Act 1972 which gives EU legislation the force of law in the UK. Speaking on Radio 4's *Today* programme the following day, Cameron said:

> I have said before that we already asserted the sovereignty of Parliament ... when we passed our Referendum Act [of 2011]. So no power can be passed from Britain to Brussels without there being a referendum, so we asserted the sovereignty. If it is necessary to do that again in more detail to make it even clearer to people that our Parliament is sovereign ... I think there is a case for it and so we will look very carefully at that.

Cameron had pledged in his Chatham House speech to examine how to emulate Germany's constitutional court, which, he said, 'reserves the right to review legal acts by European institutions and courts to check whether they remain within the scope of the EU's powers'. Michael Gove, the Justice Secretary, said in early February 2016 that it was a 'live question' as to whether the UK Supreme Court 'should be encouraged, legislated, to become a constitutional court' similar to that in Germany. However, the German court has never ruled against the EU. Speaking to The Times, Lord

Pannick QC, a human rights lawyer and cross-bench peer, said:

> For our Supreme Court to be given a function similar to that of the German constitutional court would not have any practical effect. The proposal has no legal merit. It may have a useful political purpose for the government, but the Prime Minister should be careful about raising expectations that will not be achievable.

In practice, there are several ways that control over national sovereignty has been eroded by the EU. Ever more agreements are made by QMV, meaning that in those policy areas Britain is no longer able to stop EU laws by itself. A government minister who opposes a new measure has to find enough ministers from other nations to form a blocking group, using a formula based on national population levels. It was not always like this. At the time that Britain joined, when the European club was much smaller, there was a gentleman's agreement that any one nation could call time on any proposal that affected its 'very important national interests'. But this agreement, known as the Luxembourg Compromise, could not survive the expansion of the EU and died out in the 1980s. Few decisions make it as far as a vote today because compromises are usually agreed before that stage to avoid an acrimonious showdown. Data from VoteWatch.eu on all votes by ministers at European Council meetings showed that Britain went from being in a losing minority 2.6 per cent of the time in 2004–09 to 12.3 per cent in 2009–15. making it the most frequently outvoted member nation. In March 2013, Britain lost its record of never being outvoted on a financial services policy when it failed to prevent an EU cap on bankers' bonuses. In a sign of Britain's waning influence and ability to form alliances to safeguard an area of key national importance, not one other member state sided with the UK. Qualified Majority Voting has been steadily extended even to matters of crucial national importance, such as the selection of the President of the European Commission and the settlement of the EU's annual budget. In the past, British Prime Ministers (John Major and Tony Blair) used their power of veto to blackball ardent federalists (both from Belgium) for the top job in the EU bureaucracy. Such a veto is no longer possible because the appointment was made subject to QMV by the Lisbon Treaty, along with the final decision on the EU's annual budget. Britain was outvoted for the first time on the EU budget in May 2013 when it could not prevent a majority of member nations agreeing a €7.3 billion top-up to annual spending. In June 2014, it was outvoted for the first time on the choice of a new President for the European Commission, when Britain was on the losing end of a 26–2 vote to appoint Jean-Claude Juncker of Luxembourg.

The idea of the Luxembourg Compromise was suggested by the Fresh Start group of Conservative MPs in the form of a powerful 'emergency brake' in their Mandate for Reform to guide David Cameron on the powers he should try and win back from the EU ahead of the referendum. In November 2013, they wrote:

> There is a very real issue of a sovereign government being outvoted in Brussels under Qualified Majority Voting, and a law being foisted upon a nation against the will of its government and people, and it must be addressed. An emergency brake procedure should be introduced, modelled on the so-called Luxembourg Compromise. Under this provision, a member state that considers an EU proposal to be a threat to a fundamental national interest could refer that proposal to the European Council where unanimity, and hence a national veto, would apply.

Such a move is regarded as a backwards step in Brussels that would bring decision-making to a halt by effectively making every single measure again subject to unanimity and endless negotiation. In the end, Cameron decided not to push for such sweeping powers as part of his renegotiation.

British sovereignty over making and enforcing its own laws has also been chipped away by the European Court of Justice. This body, based in Luxembourg and consisting of twenty-eight judges – one from each EU member state – is the supreme arbiter of European law, giving it a decisive say over increasing aspects of British life. Sometimes areas which are not supposed to be controlled by the EU have been ordered to change by the judges in Luxembourg. One of these was car insurance. In a ruling on gender equality in 2011 based on a test case brought by a Belgian consumer group, the ECJ judged that it was illegal to exempt car insurers from discrimination on the basis of sex. This meant that the government had to change British law by issuing a Statutory Instrument (SI 2012/2992 amending the Equality Act) to stop insurers offering lower premiums to women drivers from December 2012. Calling the ruling 'utter madness', Sajjad Karim, a Conservative MEP, said:

> It is a statistical reality that young men have more car accidents than women so it should be reflected in their premiums. Once again we have seen how an activist European Court can over-interpret the treaty. Unelected judges have overruled the will of democratically elected MEPs and governments; is it any wonder people are so disenchanted with the EU?

Another knock-on effect was on the pensions industry, where it became illegal for providers to continue their usual practice of offering higher annuity rates to men because they lived fewer years in retirement than women. The ruling was welcomed as 'an important step towards putting the fundamental right of gender equality into practice' by Viviane Reding, the EU's Justice Commissioner at the time of the ruling. 'A modern insurance company should not distinguish between women and men,' she added. Whatever one thought about the change, it was a clear example of British law being directed by the judges in Luxembourg – as a result of a court case brought by Belgium.

Concerns over the circumvention of national sovereignty were epitomised by the introduction of the Working Time Directive in 1993. Britain had opted out of the Social Chapter of the Maastricht Treaty to avoid the EU setting rules on domestic working conditions. Jacques Delors, then European Commission President, simply bypassed the Social Chapter by proposing the Working Time Directive under a different legal route, health and safety law, which was agreed by Qualified Majority Voting by eleven votes to one, with only Britain against. This legislation stipulated maximum weekly working hours as well as daily and weekly rest periods and minimum holidays. There was already an understandable sense of Britain being bumped into accepting the directive before a series of rulings by the ECJ then dramatically expanded the application of the EU law with massive extra costs to employers. The Simap judgment in 2000 added on-call time to working hours calculations; the Jaeger judgment of 2003 ruled that time spent asleep at the workplace (such as junior doctors at hospital) counted as working time; the Stringer judgment of 2009 meant that paid annual leave continued to accrue when workers were off sick, even if they were off sick all year; and the Pereda judgment of 2009 ruled that if an employee fell sick just before taking annual leave, he could take the holiday that overlapped with his sickness at a later date. The EU does not have formal powers over national healthcare systems and yet the NHS alone faced huge extra costs, with the directive blamed for much of its £1 billion annual bill for locum doctors to cover gaps in rotas. The recurring cost of the Working Time Directive to the British economy has been put at £4.2 billion a year by the Open Europe think tank.

The ECJ has long been viewed by eurosceptics as having the overtly political objective of forging greater EU integration due to its mandate not only to clarify the law but also to uphold the European treaties and their founding principle to create 'ever closer union' contained in the first line of the original Treaty of Rome of 1957. This prompted David Cameron to make disapplying 'ever closer union' to Britain one of his key renegotiation aims. 'The European treaty commits the member states to "lay the foundations of an ever closer union among the peoples of Europe",' Cameron said in his Bloomberg speech.

> This has been consistently interpreted as applying not to the peoples but rather to the states and institutions compounded by a European Court of Justice that has consistently supported greater centralisation. We understand and respect the right of others to maintain their commitment to this goal. But for Britain – and perhaps for others – it is not the objective. And we would be much more comfortable if the treaty specifically said so, freeing those who want to go further, faster, to do so, without being held back by the others.

This attempt to draw a line in the sand to protect national sovereignty found support from a founding member state, the Netherlands, which declared after its own review of EU policy that 'the time of an "ever closer union" in every possible policy area is behind us'. Some Conservative eurosceptic MPs do not believe that an opt-out from 'ever closer union' will make a material difference, however. Sir Bill Cash, a long-standing critic of the EU, asked Cameron at Prime Minister's Questions in October 2015: 'Will you recognise that even if the words "ever closer union" were to be removed from treaties for the future this will not change any of our existing EU obligations and laws, nor fundamentally change our relationship with the EU under existing treaties?' Cameron replied:

> I think the issue of ever closer union is important both symbolically and legally. Important symbolically because I think the British people always felt we were told we were joining a common market and we were never really told enough about this political union which we've never been happy with. I want to make it explicit that for us it is principally a common market and not an ever closer union. But it does have legal force because ever closer union has been used by the courts to enforce centralising judgments and I want that to change.

Leaving the EU would not necessarily see sovereignty fully restored to Parliament, however. Partly that is because, as explored in later chapters, no country can exist in isolation from the international rules that govern cross-border activities like finance, trade, travel and transportation. Partly it is also because the UK will not become completely detached from Europe in the event of Brexit. As discussed in the Democracy chapter, if the UK wants to stay fully inside the Single Market after leaving the EU it will have to be in the European Economic Area like Norway. While this will restore national sovereignty over agriculture, fisheries, justice and home affairs, regional funding and trade, Parliament would have to agree to accept all EU laws related to the Single Market without having a decisive say over them. Outside the EEA, if Britain tried something like the Swiss system of bilateral deals with Brussels on different areas of interest like trade and air travel, this would offer a greater return to national sovereignty, although in practice many international standards for activities like farming, consumer protection and the environment would still be set in Brussels without British input.

You have to go all the way back to Harold Macmillan to find a Prime Minister prepared to explain candidly what joining the European club would really mean for British sovereignty. 'It is true of course that political unity is the central aim of those European countries and we would naturally accept that ultimate goal,' he wrote in a pamphlet in 1962, setting out his reasons for making Britain's first, unsuccessful, application for membership. 'In renouncing some of our own sovereignty we would receive in return a share of the sovereignty renounced by other members.' The most eloquent modern explanation of why it makes sense to share sovereignty to achieve national goals in today's more complicated world and much larger European Union came from a judicial source. The life story of Sir Konrad Schiemann, Britain's former judge at the European Court of Justice, owes much to the peaceful system of European cooperation created after the Second World War, a conflict which left him an orphan in his native Berlin. Brought by an uncle to grow up in England, he studied at Cambridge, became a High Court judge and rose to the pinnacle of British society as a member of the Privy Council. 'We no longer live in a time when the military and economic might of the UK was such that the government could hope to achieve whatever it desired by threats. Gunboat diplomacy has gone,' Schiemann wrote in an essay for Regent's University in 2013.

> The achievement of our national aims requires the cooperation of other governments, just as the achievement of their national aims requires our cooperation. We cannot all do exactly what we want, because we do not all want the same things. Progress is made by giving up one desideratum in order to achieve another. This involves making choices difficult for all parties – a task which is made impossible if each party relies on a concept of sovereignty which implies that it must be free of all constraints and allowed to do whatever it wants.

Schiemann argued that it would be inefficient and ineffective to withdraw from multilateral bodies like the EU and try to achieve national aims by negotiating bilaterally with every country on every issue. 'The structure of the EU is designed to facilitate the inevitable compromises,' he wrote, dismissing the idea of a wide-ranging 'emergency brake' to pull out of unwanted policies.

> For shared sovereignty to be effectively exercised requires mutual trust and mutual commitment. If you wish to obtain the certainty that your partner will be bound by the agreement even when he or she finds it inconvenient, then you have to live with the fact that you must agree to be bound by it even when you find it inconvenient.

Schiemann appealed for debate about sovereignty to be rooted in the real world where some countries are more powerful than others and all have their own national interests. Even the most powerful cannot achieve everything they want without cooperating with others.

> A state's domestic law may permit it to export sausages with a large bread content, or beer with a small hop content, or indeed nuclear detritus or other refuse. But this is of no practical value unless other states permit the import of those goods. So mutual agreement has to be reached ... A state's domestic laws may limit radiation emissions or prescribe air quality of a particular purity, but this is of limited practical value if emissions or air of inferior quality comes in from the state next door. So equivalent standards are desirable. A state may wish to encourage its companies to establish subsidiaries in other states, but this is of little practical value unless the other states in question allow the establishment of such subsidiaries. So mutual recognition is required.

The major achievement of the EU has been setting up a mechanism for arriving at policy decisions which bind everyone, he concluded.

> You have to take the rough with the smooth, and you have to accept compromise ... The most effective way for the UK to achieve what it wishes to achieve is by seeking to persuade others that they are likely to achieve more of what they want if they do not stand in the way of the UK achieving what it wants. This is more easily done within the EU than outside it. If we are outside, those countries inside will devote their energies to doing deals with their partners inside the Union and are likely – politely or less politely – to ignore us.

Schiemann is persuasive – that's his job as an advocate. But the key issue for many British voters is that the EU has gone too far and claimed too much jurisdiction over national life. Subsidiarity – the EU's technical term for power being exercised at the appropriate local, national or European level – was established in the Maastricht Treaty of 1993 but has never been rigorously applied to devolve decision-making. Instead, Brussels empire builders have grabbed national sovereignty in a game of thrones that many Europeans, not just the British, feel they did not sign up for. Schiemann's eloquent argument for pooling sovereignty cannot be faulted for its logic, only for its application. The impact of the European Union's ever-widening range of powers over national life causes legitimate concerns about the sacrifice of sovereignty that is demanded and touches on deep feelings of national identity. Brussels also wields power in sectors where it formally has little, for example in healthcare with the huge costs to the NHS of the Working Time Directive. The one-way transfer of sovereignty also causes alarm that a power-hungry central authority is competing with national parliaments in a zero sum game rather than cooperating with them. This is why David Cameron focused on boosting national sovereignty as one of the four key aims of his renegotiation ahead of the referendum. At the same time, nobody can argue for complete sovereignty in today's inter-connected world, where compromises have to be struck internationally to enable global systems of finance, travel and trade to function. The question is the degree to which Britain needs to be committed to integration with the EU to achieve national goals. Opinion polls suggested that a convincing package of safeguards to protect national sovereignty would help convince voters to remain in the EU, whereas the prospect of ever more accumulation of power in Brussels – and Luxembourg – will push the UK away.[30]

One other core aspect of the United Kingdom's sovereignty could dramatically change as a result of the EU referendum. The Scottish National Party has made it clear that if Scotland voted to remain while across the UK as a whole there was a majority for leaving, then it would expect a second referendum on Scottish independence, following its rejection by 55.3 per cent to 44.7 per cent in 2014. Nicola Sturgeon, the SNP leader and First Minister of Scotland, told BBC1's *The Andrew Marr Show* in January 2016:

> If Scotland had voted to stay in and the UK as a whole votes to come out, which therefore means Scotland faces being taken out of the EU when we don't want to be, I have said before and I will say again, I think it is highly likely that would trigger an overwhelming demand for a second Scottish referendum on independence. The democratic outrage of being taken out of Europe against our will I think would make that almost inevitable.

This presents a conundrum for British voters who base their objections to the EU on its threat to the integrity of national sovereignty. A vote to leave could unleash forces that tear apart an independent Britain before it has had a chance to assert its new-found freedom. Even if Scotland does not leave the UK in the event of Brexit, the Scottish Parliament could refuse to reject or revise EU laws in the same way as the Westminster Parliament, setting the two bodies up for a long constitutional battle.

TRADE

IN The EU has sole responsibility for negotiating international trade agreements on behalf of its twenty-eight members and has concluded recent deals with Canada, Singapore, South Korea and Vietnam, with the big prizes of the US, Japan and India in the pipeline. No tariffs or quotas apply to goods moving between EU states and a common tariff is applied to goods entering from outside.

OUT Britain can negotiate its own preferential trade agreements, take up its own seat at the World Trade Organization, regain the power to decide its own import duties and explore a wider Commonwealth trading deal. It could continue to deal on preferential terms with the EU through a Free Trade Agreement, or on the same terms as a full member if it is in the European Economic Area.

KEY STATS The EU is by far Britain's biggest trading partner, accounting for 44.6 per cent of UK goods and services exports (£226.7 billion) in 2014 and 53.2 per cent of imports (£288.3 billion).[31] Britain's next biggest trading partner is the US with £87.9 billion of exports and £50.8 billion of imports in 2014.[32] Britain has a large trade deficit in goods, with imports from the EU exceeding exports by £77 billion in 2014.[33] For UK exporters and importers, Germany is the main EU partner followed by Netherlands and France.

Lye Cross Farm's premium cheese made by Alvis Brothers of north Somerset sits at a constant temperature of 8–12°C in their warehouse for a year to replicate the same gentle ageing conditions of the famous local caves originally used to store and mature cheddar. The company combines traditional methods with a very modern approach to sales which saw exports grow from 4 to 25 per cent of their output in just a few years. Not only do they sell cheese to the French but Lye Cross Farm is also a big hit in South Korea, where sales were up 50 per cent in 2012 following the country's free trade agreement with the EU the previous year. Tim Harrap, the company's head of collaboration, puts the export success down to a combination of factors, including the appeal of the Union Jack on the wrapper and trade fairs run by UK Trade & Industry (UKTI), the government's trade promotion body, as well as personal contacts. But he gives the main credit for being able to break into international markets to the European Union, not just to the Single Market but to its food quality schemes, particularly the Protected Designation of Origin (PDO) label, awarded to Lye Cross Farm for their West Country Farmhouse Cheddar, verifying its authenticity and provenance. This gave it extra kudos in the status-obsessed Far East market. 'Korea is a great place as there is a strong interest in Britain and its culture, so the UK's imported products are much sought after by consumers,' said Harrap. 'The biggest driver of this was the European Union–South Korea Free Trade Agreement. Although the tariffs on cheese were not cut straight away they are reducing over the years. We are up against the New Zealand product but there was no free trade agreement between New Zealand and South Korea until December 2015.' Harrap has travelled extensively promoting British cheese as part of UK and EU trade missions around the globe, having watched other local cheddar producers that did not diversify into foreign sales go out of business. Export success for him depends on a combination of British pluck and EU muscle. 'It seems to me that whilst the British are navel gazing the world is moving on apace – we cannot afford to pull up the drawbridge.'

In the twenty years before Britain joined the EEC in 1973, the proportion of UK trade (total of imports and exports) with the original six member nations rose from 13 to 21 per cent. In the twenty years following accession, British trade with these six countries more than doubled to 44 per cent.[34] This was hardly surprising given the thousands of common standards and rules adopted by the member states to smooth trade between them, as well as the common external tariff to deter competition from outside their Customs Union. An internal UK government paper released under Freedom of Information rules from 2005 put the boost of EU membership for trade between member states at 40 per cent while the loss of trade with countries outside the EU due to its Customs Union was said to be 5 per cent.[35] The question now, however, is whether it is time to refocus elsewhere given Europe's relatively low growth prospects compared to other parts of the world. In an article in *The Times* in May 2013 explaining why he would vote to leave the EU, the former Chancellor of the Exchequer Lord Lawson argued that the general lowering of global tariffs and other barriers through successive rounds of World Trade Organization liberalisation now made EU membership unnecessary from a trade perspective. To make his point, he said that UK exports to the EU had risen in cash terms by 40 per cent over the decade but that exports to the EU from countries outside it had gone up by 75 per cent. 'The heart of the matter is that the relevant economic context nowadays is not Europe but globalisation, including global free trade, with the World Trade Organization as its monitor,' he concluded. He also warned that British businesses were too focused on Europe, a continent in slow decline, and were therefore missing great export opportunities in the developing world, especially Asia. The EU had served its 'historic purpose' and was now 'past its sell-by date', he argued. The facts bear out Lawson's case on the EU's inward-looking approach to trade. In the Mercosur group of nations in South America, 16 per cent of exports are to each other and 84 per cent further afield; in the Asean group of countries in South East Asia, 25 per cent of exports are within the region; and in Nafta in North America (US, Canada and Mexico) 51 per cent are inter-regional.[36] In the EU, meanwhile, 65 per cent of exporting is between member nations. This over-reliance on intra-EU trade comes at a time of general economic decline both in absolute terms and relative to the rest of the world. Europe's share of world merchandise trade has fallen from its peak of 50.9 per cent in 1973 to 45.4 per cent in 1993 and 36.4 per cent in 2013.[37]

Lye Cross Farm, however, is one British business that owes much not just to the EU's Single Market but also to its sole responsibility for negotiating pref-erential Free Trade Agreements (FTAs) with countries and regions further afield. The FTA with South Korea,

which came into force in July 2011, had an immediate impact on British trade. UK goods exports to the
world's fifteenth-largest economy grew by 82 per cent in
2012 to £4.9 billion and services grew by 5 per cent to
£1.5 billion.[38] The South Korea FTA was the most extensive trade deal ever struck by the EU at the time and came
after a 'lost decade' when Brussels was more focused on
trying to secure a global trade liberalisation agreement
under the WTO's Doha Round of talks that began in
2001. While these negotiations were stalled for years,
other developed trading nations like the United States
and Australia pushed on with making FTAs that fuelled
frustration among eurosceptics at the apparent inaction
of the European Commission and led to trade becoming
a key argument in favour of leaving the EU. In the same
time that the EU managed only one modern FTA with
South Korea, New Zealand concluded eight trade deals
including with China, Malaysia and Thailand. 'We don't
want to be stuck inside a Customs Union that prohibits
us from making our own trade deals with the rest of the
world – the growing parts of the world,' Nigel Farage
told UKIP's annual conference in 2012.

After the renegotiation of a simple free trade deal with
the European Union, we would like to see Britain thinking
bigger. There is a group of countries out there that represent nearly a third of the population of the globe, where
they speak English, have common law, are our real friends
in the world. We would like to extend free trade to include
the Commonwealth. That is the way forward.

If Britain were to leave the EU, its first port of call for new trading relationships would be the so-called Anglosphere (basically, the Commonwealth plus the US). As UKIP policy stated:

> UKIP will seek to establish a Commonwealth Free Trade Area (CFTA) with the fifty-three other Commonwealth countries. The Commonwealth Business Council estimates that a CFTA would account for more than 20 per cent of all international trade and investment, facilitating annual trade exchanges worth more than $1.8 trillion and direct foreign investment worth about $100 billion. Yet the Commonwealth has been shamefully betrayed and neglected by previous governments. Commonwealth nations share a common language, legal and democratic systems, account for a third of the world's population and a quarter of its trade, with the average age of a citizen just twenty-five years. India, for example, will soon become the second largest world economy and Britain should not be tied to the dead political weight of the European Union, but retain its own friendly trading and cultural links.

Europe is getting older and growing less, both economically and demographically, than the rest of the world. The EU had two countries among the world's most populous twenty nations in 2000: Germany in twelfth place with 82.3 million and France in twentieth place with 59.3 million. The Commonwealth had four in the top ten: India in second place with 1.02 billion people;

Pakistan seventh with 142.7 million; Bangladesh eighth with 138 million; and Nigeria tenth with 114.7 million. By 2050 there are forecast to be no current EU countries among the world's biggest twenty, although Turkey makes nineteenth place with 97.8 million people. India will become the world's most populous country with 1.53 billion inhabitants and the Commonwealth will have five in the top twenty: Pakistan fourth; Nigeria sixth; Bangladesh seventh; and Uganda seventeenth.[39]

The World Economics organisation found in 2012 that the Commonwealth's share of global GDP had already overtaken that of Britain's major partners in Europe. Their researchers plotted real terms GDP and growth for the eight nations (excluding the UK) which have been members of the EU since 1973, and compared it to the growth rate for Commonwealth countries and also with the eurozone. They found that the Commonwealth had come from a long way behind to outperform the EU8 in terms of share of world GDP and was poised to do the same with the eurozone. Real terms average annual growth for the eurozone was forecast to rise by 2.7 per cent from 2012 until 2017 and for the Commonwealth by 7.3 per cent, using International Monetary Fund figures. 'Whilst joining the EU may have been a good thing for the UK for a number of reasons, it is clear that in sheer market growth terms, the Commonwealth is proving the more dynamic economic grouping,' said World Economics. 'The potential for future market growth appears very limited in the EU, whereas the potential is still vast in the Commonwealth.'

Population growth in the Commonwealth is set to be twice as rapid as in the eurozone up until 2050.

The trouble with the 53-nation Commonwealth is that it is a grouping of economies of different scales and stages of development, with no single representative with whom to negotiate a free trade deal. Ransford Smith, Deputy Secretary General (Economic) of the Commonwealth from 2006 to 2012, believes there were too many hurdles to a comprehensive Commonwealth Free Trade Agreement because most of its countries were still developing the infrastructure and administrative systems necessary to compete internationally. 'The real objective of these countries is to trade with the most competitive source and build the capacity to trade … It is about transforming more Commonwealth countries into the Singapores and Malaysias and doing that does not mean those countries should become more closely interlinked with the UK.'

The Commonwealth would not be the only option available to Britain if it left the EU and was free to make its own global trade deals again. The other obvious place to look would be across the Atlantic to North America, where Canada, Mexico and the US concluded the North American Free Trade Agreement (Nafta) in 1994. The benefits in terms of increased trade were huge in the following decade, leading some Republican politicians to suggest that the UK could also benefit by joining. *The Economist* noted that Nafta looked just like the sort of arrangement that Britain always wanted the EU to be, i.e. 'a giant free-trade area linking sovereign countries, without any common body of law, or any notion of developing a common foreign policy'. The only snag, the magazine added, was that the UK signed over its ability to negotiate entry into Nafta when it joined the EU.

While an independent UK would be much smaller than the EU and have less clout in international trade negotiations on its own, it would not be a minnow. It is the world's eighth largest merchandise exporter, with $542 billion worth in 2013, a quarter the value of China's and a third the value of the US's. Britain is the sixth biggest importer of goods, with $655 billion, behind the US, China, Germany, Japan and France. But when it comes to the trade in commercial services, the UK actually exports more in dollar value than China, $293 billion compared to $205 billion, putting it in second place behind the US.[40] In recent years, however, the case for Britain leaving the EU to make Free Trade Agreements of its own has weakened. That is because the European Commission finally accepted the futility of chasing the Doha world deal and set out an ambitious programme of its own, following the South Korea FTA with Colombia and Peru, and reaching provisional agreement in 2013 with Singapore and Canada, the latter forecast to increase bilateral trade in goods and services by a fifth to €25.7 billion a year. The British economy is estimated to benefit from the Canada deal by £1.3 billion a year.

A trade agreement with the US would stimulate European GDP by €65 billion, with Japan by €43 billion and with India by €3.8 billion, the Commission forecast, with further significant productivity gains to follow. As a trading nation, Britain, with 11.5 per cent of all EU exports and 14.5 per cent of EU imports, could expect to benefit disproportionately from this potential wind-fall. In its new trade and investment strategy unveiled in October 2015, the EU also outlined plans to begin FTA talks with Commonwealth members Australia and New Zealand, as well as the Philippines and Indonesia. In January 2016 it announced a consultation on whether to give market economy status to China, which would open the door to more cheap imports. Success in these ambitions would negate a big part of the argument for British withdrawal, namely that the EU is too sclerotic and inward-looking to conclude better deals than Britain could achieve on its own. The real potential game-changer in the trade argument is the proposed deal with the US, known as the Transatlantic Trade and Investment Partnership (TTIP), which is why David Cameron was so keen to stand alongside President Obama to announce the start of the talks in July 2013. TTIP was forecast to boost UK exports to the US by between 1.2 and 2.9 per cent, benefit the British econ-omy by between £4 billion and £10 billion a year, and set down regulatory benchmarks for the rest of the world.[41] A further argument in favour of sticking with the EU is the view both within the European Commission and the UK government's Department for Business, Innovation and Skills that Britain would not automatically be able to continue with the Free Trade Deals negotiated on its behalf by the EU if it were to end its membership. John Clancy, EU Trade spokesman, said:

If a country leaves the EU, European law becomes inapplicable. This includes trade agreements between the EU and third countries. The UK would therefore not benefit from any preference granted by a third state to the EU. Reversely the UK would be free to define its own external customs tariff with all third countries.

Phil Hogan, the EU agriculture commissioner, told the 2016 Oxford Farming Conference:

How would Britain, with a population of 60 million, fare in negotiating with countries like China, with a population of 1.3 billion? In the EU it punches at a weight of 500 million, almost twice the size of the US. It could take years to negotiate deals with Korea, Canada and so on – deals the EU has already successfully negotiated.

If Britain were to leave the EU, it could regain its international trade mandate and stay inside the Single Market by following Norway into the European Economic Area (EEA). If the EEA was rejected, then Britain would try for a Free Trade Agreement with the EU like Switzerland, preferably with access for both goods and services. This could be overseen by something similar to the Trade Committee for the EU–South Korea FTA which has fifteen members, five from each side and five neutrals, as well as six specialised committees of experts in particular fields: trade in goods, sanitary and phytosanitary, customs, trade in services, sustainable development, and outward processing zones. There are also seven sectoral working groups. Instead of the European Court of Justice (ECJ), there is a system of consultations to resolve disputes and failing that, matters go before a three-person arbitration panel, made up of members of the Trade Committee chaired by one of the independents. That is quite a reduction from the ECJ with its 1,991 staff and its 2014 annual budget of €355 million.[42]

If no FTA was agreed, however, Britain's trading relationship with the EU would then be based on the general rules of the World Trade Organization. It would not mean exorbitant new tariffs for all British exporters although some sectors would suffer badly. Cars would face a 10 per cent import duty, for example, as discussed in the Investment chapter, in the unlikely event that pressure from the German government in support of its exporters did not prevail. The arguments for keeping close trading links with the EU are many and varied, and generally accepted by eurosceptics. Campaigners for Brexit argue that there is little prospect of a complete breakdown in relations and so a preferential UK-EU FTA is a strong likelihood, given the present close and mutually advantageous trading relationship. Daniel Hannan, a Conservative MEP and one of the most persuasive campaigners for Britain to pull out of the EU, wrote:

I have yet to meet a British eurosceptic who wants to withdraw from the European market. Such people may exist but, in all the years that I've campaigned against the current system, I've never come across them. What eurosceptics want, rather, is to withdraw from the EU's political structures while retaining trade links – along the lines of what Switzerland does, though with some modifications. This point is worth stressing, because supporters of EU membership have taken to arguing against a proposition that no one is seriously suggesting, namely the idea that Britain, a maritime and mercantile nation, should cut all ties to her European allies ... It is sometimes suggested that, if Britain withdrew from the EU's political structures, it would face economic sanctions from the other members. I don't believe it: trade barriers would be self-defeating. In 2013, the UK overtook France to become Germany's single biggest export destination. We run a structural trade deficit with the EU (though not with the rest of the world), buying more than we sell. On the day we left the customs union, we would become easily its largest market, larger than the second and third largest (the US and Japan) combined. Why would anyone want to restrict cross-channel trade?

The UK's large trade deficit with the EU (UK imports exceeded exports by £61.6 billion in 2014) means that the continent would have more to lose in a trade war than Britain. But if Britain was outside the EU and EEA, agreement on free trade with the member states on services would be less certain than for goods. Within the overall trade deficit in 2014, the UK ran a surplus in services meaning that exports were £15.4 billion more than imports, giving the EU less of an incentive to agree a free trade deal on services – as discussed further in the chapter on the City – which in turn could harm the British economy given the size of its service sector. The government has said that British GDP could be boosted by up to 7 per cent by 'completing the Single Market' in services by breaking down the EU's remaining internal trade barriers. On the one hand, it is an indictment of the resistance to market opening in EU countries that much still remains to be done on things like the recognition of professional qualifications to open up competition on services. On the other hand, it is another argument in favour of Britain staying inside the EU to push for reform rather than leaving and removing pressure on recalcitrant governments across the Channel to give UK services a better chance to compete for business there.

SECTORS

THE CITY AND FINANCE

IN London is the undisputed financial centre of the EU despite the UK staying out of the euro. A strong British voice at the table during decisions on laws proposed by the European Commission and amended by MEPs helps to protect the City's competitiveness.

OUT Free of EU controls, the City could become an offshore financial centre to Europe like Singapore or Hong Kong to Asia. But if the UK fails to retain complete access to the Single Market for financial services, there could be an exodus of international players from London.

KEY STATS Britain has a 70 per cent market share of financial services in Europe. 78 per cent of all foreign exchange trades in the EU and 85 per cent of hedge fund management takes place in the City. Financial services accounted for 7.9 per cent of UK GDP and 11.5 per cent of tax receipts, worth £66 billion, in 2013–14.[43]

When a Frenchman was appointed as European Commissioner for the Single Market and Financial Services for the first time in fifty years, Nicolas Sarkozy, the French President, declared that the British were 'the big losers' in the five-yearly carve-up of top EU jobs in 2009. 'I want the world to see the victory of the European model, which has nothing to do with the excesses of financial capitalism,' said Sarkozy, who blamed the global economic crisis on the 'free-wheeling Anglo-Saxon' model of financial market practices. Michel Barnier, the former French Foreign Minister chosen for the commissioner role, was quick to try and reassure a nervous City of London over fears that he would unleash a barrage of EU legislation not merely to clip its wings but to bring it down. 'I plan to work with everybody. I'm not an ideologist. I'm very practical. Everybody needs to calm down,' he said. A British eurocrat was installed as director-general of Barnier's department to ease government concerns. Five years on, Barnier's directorate had produced one of the most extensive legislative programmes ever seen in one term of a European Commissioner but many of the new laws were limited to the nations in the eurozone. Much of the legislation and policy was aimed at preventing a repeat of the near break-up of the euro in 2010–12 and Britain ensured that it opted out of the most demanding calls on national sovereignty made in the proposed EU Banking Union. These included the Single Supervisory Mechanism under the European Central Bank to keep an eye on the biggest banks in the eurozone and the Single Resolution Mechanism for winding up a failing eurozone bank. A host of other measures were also brought in for all twenty-eight EU nations, however. Measures for closer supervision and annual recommendations by the European Commission about national budgets in the European Semester programme, led to the extraordinary spectacle of the Irish Budget being sent to Brussels and discussed in the finance committee of the German Bundestag before it reached the floor of the Dáil. Again, Britain kept some distance from this policy by refusing to hand over details of its Budget until Parliament heard them first.

Although many in the City grumbled about extra controls and safeguards, Barnier was not the monster some had feared. The real problem that emerged during his tenure for the UK was the growing realisation that the euro club was growing in regulatory strength. Far from losing members as seemed possible during the height of the euro crisis – with huge bailout loans provided to Greece, Portugal, Ireland and Cyprus in return for drastic economic reforms – Latvia joined the Single Currency in 2014, Lithuania in 2015, and others are queuing up to follow them. This will only increase their tendency to club together to back EU legislation and policy primarily to benefit their own interests. Of the twenty-eight EU members, only the UK and Denmark have treaty-based opt-outs from the euro, although Sweden is likely to avoid joining for the foreseeable future. Even without any new members, the nineteen eurozone countries have an unbeatable qualified majority to win votes in the European Council under new rules from the Lisbon Treaty stipulating that a decision can only pass with 55 per cent of the members and 65 per cent of the EU population (the eurozone had 65.9 per cent in 2014).

David Cameron's first stab at protecting the UK's financial services industry from a eurozone caucus was a spectacular flop. The Prime Minister told an EU summit in December 2011 that he wanted several safeguards in exchange for agreeing to the Fiscal Compact, a new set of German-inspired economic rules to limit national debts and deficits aimed mainly at eurozone countries. The other EU leaders refused, partly because not enough time was spent building up allies around the table before the meeting, and partly because the details were not seen as directly relevant to the subject in hand, namely the coordination of national budgets. The rest of the EU, with the exception of the Czech Republic, simply ignored Cameron and went ahead with a treaty between themselves to implement the Fiscal Compact, vowing to make it full EU law by 2018. Cameron's failed repatriation of powers was essentially about restoring a veto to financial services regulation. In common with many aspects of the Single Market, the veto was replaced with Qualified Majority Voting to speed up decision-making and overcome vested national interests under rule changes agreed to by Margaret Thatcher. But Cameron had support from the industry for his tough stance – 70 per cent of managers at UK finance firms told a poll in December 2011 that they agreed with the statement: 'The UK government needs to renegotiate existing EU treaties to safeguard the City of London, limiting agreements to trade and association only.'[44]

Britain's next attempt at protecting the City from hostile eurozone-inspired laws was much more successful. During negotiations for the first stage of a Banking Union for the eurozone in December 2012, giving the European Central Bank responsibility for supervising the biggest banks in the Single Currency area, George Osborne secured a new 'double-majority' system for decisions by the European Banking Authority, the organisation that regulates most, smaller, EU banks. When a new rule is agreed, there will have to be a majority by voting weight of all EU members, plus a simple unweighted majority of the eurozone 'outs' and 'ins'. If a majority of the eurozone 'outs' do not like a new banking rule, they can block it. As Robert Peston of the BBC said on his blog:

> Although this double-majority voting system for the EBA sounds boringly procedural, it could prove to be very significant. It could provide an important blueprint to preserve the UK's voting voice and weight on the future of the Single Market, as and when the eurozone evolves into an even more unified political bloc. It implies that the UK might be able to co-exist in the European Union with a currency union that becomes a political union.

This proved prescient, as one of Cameron's four key renegotiation demands ahead of the referendum was for a double-majority system of protection for non-eurozone countries like Britain against block voting by eurozone nations. Cameron secured this in his draft renegotiation agreement with Donald Tusk, President of the European Council, subject to further talks on the scope of the new power and the number of non-eurozone nations required to query a decision by the single currency countries. The draft agreement also established the important principles that 'measures … to deepen the economic and monetary union will be voluntary for member states whose currency is not the euro', while emergency moves to shore up the euro, such as the huge loans for struggling states like Greece 'will not entail budgetary responsibility for the non-eurozone countries'. These were measures which sought to address the concerns of Mark Carney, Governor of the Bank of England, who said in a speech broadly supportive of EU membership in October 2015 that it was 'desirable' for 'clear principles to safeguard the interests of non-euro member states'.

There are two schools of thought for what happens to the City in the event of Brexit. One is the majority view that global companies, which chose London partly because it is the world's largest trading centre for the euro with access to the Single Market, would relocate much of their operation inside the EU. The other is that we have heard all this before at the launch of the euro in 2000, when there was a lot of paranoia fuelled by claims that the new currency would mean the demise of the City. It proved to be far from the case, with twice as many euros traded in London in 2012 as in the whole of the rest of the eurozone. One senior City figure said:

> It is possible that London, being outside the EU, could still survive as an offshore financial centre in the way that Singapore is a major centre or Hong Kong outside mainstream China. It is not clear if being outside would be the death knell for London, but it would certainly not be as beneficial as being on the inside.

There are undoubtedly parts of the EU system, including many MEPs and some member states, which are hostile to the 'Anglo-Saxon model' of capitalism or want to claim back some of the euro business conducted in the City. A European Central Bank policy paper in 2011 demanded that clearing houses, another key part of City life, should be based in the eurozone if they handle more than 5 per cent of the market in a euro-denominated financial product. The British government immediately took the ECB to the European Court of Justice to protect the City. Otherwise the ECB demands would force a partial relocation away from the City of LCH. Clearnet, one of the world's largest clearing houses, which processes most of the share trading on the London Stock Exchange and operates a derivatives clearing service. It was a challenge to the dominance of the City that could be met with action in the European Court of Justice on the grounds of fair competition in the EU – not a legal avenue open to Britain on the outside.

There are two powerful reasons for the City staying inside both the Single Market and the EU. One is the familiar argument that Britain will lose a voice at the table when making the rules, even if it followed Norway into the European Economic Area in order to stay inside the Single Market. The advantage of full membership was shown in November 2014 when Cameron's nomination for Britain's European Commissioner, Baron Hill of Oareford, succeeded Barnier and was handed the remodelled portfolio for 'Financial Stability, Financial Services and Capital Markets Union'. One of his key tasks, to create the Capital Markets Union, is designed to open up financial services across the EU to diversify sources of investment for business away from banks.

Britain still rarely gets outvoted on financial services issues – the first time in forty years of membership was in March 2013 when George Osborne, the Chancellor, failed in his attempt to block an EU cap on bankers' bonuses of twice annual salary. The other argument is that only an EU or EEA member state can provide the financial services 'passport' necessary for companies based in that country to do business in every other EU country. Large international banks, including from non-Single Market member Switzerland, base themselves in the City of London for this reason. Without this ability, London-based banks and other organisations from the US, China and Japan would need to relocate to another member state to get the passport to do business in the EU nations. If the UK was not in the Single Market, British banks or insurance firms or hedge funds would need a passport from another EU country, which would mean a sizeable presence would probably be required in that country.

TheCityUK, an independent body that represents the financial sector, analysed the sources of the £61 billion tax take from the financial services industry in 2008–09 and identified three main groups in terms of who might stay or go if Britain quit the EU. The largest group was of domestic financial services providers, generating £35–41 billion in tax, who would find it 'hard to impossible to leave' the UK; the second group was 'sticky but not unmovable', mostly major international banks which contributed £17–22 billion in tax; the third category with 'lowest hurdles to departure' consisted of highly paid foreign nationals and international finance firms headquartered in the City out of convenience, contributing £3 billion. 'We found that the internationally mobile cohort accounts for up to £25 billion of the tax take to the Treasury,' said Chris Cummings, CEO of TheCityUK.

> The reason why these firms stay is not because of the domestic market of 63 million but because they want access to the European market of 440 million. Once an institution from the US, China or Japan decide they want to be in Europe the question is, where is the best place to be based. That comes down to a fight between Paris, Frankfurt and London. The time zone, language, skills base and cluster factor of all these firms here benefit the City.

TheCityUK believes Britain is better off staying inside the Single Market for financial services and this is 'nothing to do with politics, simply the money', Cummings added. John McFarlane, chairman of Barclays and of TheCityUK, said that a survey of the group's members found 85 per cent wanted to remain in the EU, while 4 per cent favoured leaving. 'Our opinion is that the City will be significantly worse' because 'the rest of the world wants Britain to remain in the EU', McFarlane told Bloomberg Television in January 2016. 'Foreign organisations use London as their main access to Europe, and we don't know what the impact of withdrawal will be.'

The British Bankers' Association has called for the

government to get more involved in the EU to steer legislation. It believes that the benefits of EU membership outweigh the annoyances of regulation. 'The Single Market in financial services has been an essential ingredient in the creation of the global financial centre which London now is,' said Anthony Browne, chief executive of the BBA.

> For a lot of businesses in the City, it [leaving the EU] would be utterly devastating. It depends what 'out' looks like. If we end up still being part of the Single Market and somehow contributing to the rules of the Single Market while not being an EU member then it does not really matter. But if you stop being part of the Single Market and lose the ability to 'passport' activities then it will make it very difficult for a lot of the businesses operating in the City to deliver their services to customers across Europe. They would have to apply for reauthorisation in an EU country. The political reality is if the UK left then I am sure there would be so much political momentum particularly in France and Germany to put up barriers to London businesses selling their services across Europe. I just cannot see that they would tolerate all the financial services business going to London.

Citigroup, the huge US bank, issued its own warning in 2013 that there was 'mounting concern' among its clients about their ability to continue using the UK as a regional hub if it left the EU. Another US giant, Goldman Sachs, went further, warning that it would 'drastically reduce' its activities in London and move large numbers of jobs to Germany and France if Britain left the European Union. The American bank uses London as its European main hub, employing 5,500 people at Fleet Street compared with 200 in Frankfurt and 100 in Paris. Michael Sherwood, the bank's co-chief executive in Europe, said: 'In all likelihood we would transfer a substantial part of our European business from London to a eurozone location – the most obvious contenders being Paris and Frankfurt.' In the event of Brexit, Dublin is also seen as a potential destination for other City firms like asset managers with large portfolios in the EU that want to retain the benefits of timezone and language. Leaving the EU and its Single Market will probably diminish the role of the City and reduce its earning power for the UK, at least in the short to medium term – and could even lead to a rebalancing of the British economy away from its reliance on financial services.

DEFENCE AND SECURITY

IN British Armed Forces take part in missions organised under the EU Common Security and Defence Policy such as Atalanta to protect ships from Somalian pirates. A British ambassador attends the twice-weekly Political and Security Committee meetings in Brussels. The UK strongly resists the creation of an EU military operations HQ or an EU army.

OUT Britain can build on its strong military cooperation with France, the only other major armed power in the EU, and coordinate with European allies through NATO. UK post-war security has always been based on NATO and the 'Five Eyes' pact to share intelligence with the US, Canada, Australia and New Zealand.

KEY STATS EU nations have more military personnel than the US and are second only to China with 5.4 million active or reserve forces. The UK and France make up half the military capacity of all EU states and carry out 70 per cent of the EU spending on military research and development. At 2 per cent of GDP in 2014, UK military spending is the second largest in the EU after France; the US spends 3.5 per cent of GDP.

In one of the most embarrassing security breaches of the post-war era, it was revealed in 2013 that the Chancellor of Germany's private phone had been bugged for many years by foreign agents. The spies were not from an enemy power, however, but from the United States of America, one of Germany's key international allies. Details emerged from the whistle-blower Edward Snowden just days after President Obama had been welcomed in Berlin by Angela Merkel for private discussions and a speech in front of the Brandenburg Gate. Obama's visit was timed to commemorate the fiftieth anniversary of President Kennedy's historic visit to West Berlin when he memorably declared himself at one with the German struggle for freedom. As a symbol of close friendship, the US had been allowed to build its embassy right next door to the historic columned gateway in the heart of Berlin, just a stone's throw from the new Chancellery building. A secret listening post on top of that embassy was allegedly involved in eavesdropping on Merkel's calls on behalf of the US National Security Agency (NSA). At an EU summit in October 2013 to discuss Snowden's disclosure that the NSA routinely captured data on millions of phone calls and emails across Europe, not to mention Mrs Merkel's private conversations and possibly those of the Italian Prime Minister too, David Cameron was strangely taciturn as a joint statement was agreed. 'Cameron was present at the discussion. He listened to it. He wasn't against it. That is silent acquiescence as far as I go,' was how Merkel described the British Prime Minister's clear discomfort. The next day, *L'Espresso* newspaper claimed that British intelligence cooperated with the Americans to spy on the Italian government. Cameron refused to respond to allegations that GCHQ, the British intelligence and security organisation, assisted in NSA surveillance and signed a statement from all twenty-eight leaders acknowledging 'deep concerns among European citizens' at the NSA revelations, warning that

'a lack of trust could prejudice the necessary cooperation in the field of intelligence gathering'. The Snowden
leaks revealed, however, the existence of a secret GCHQ
operation called Tempora, which gathered huge volumes
of material from transatlantic fibre optic cables carrying
data to and from Western Europe. This information was
reportedly shared with the NSA.

A clear faultline had been dramatically exposed in
Europe's security cooperation by Snowden which had
actually been there all along. Britain and the US signed
a top secret deal to share intelligence material in 1946,
later joined by Canada, Australia and New Zealand – the
English-speaking Second World War allies. The existence
of the agreement, informally known as 'Five Eyes' after the
classification 'AUS/CAN/NZ/UK/US EYES ONLY', was
not publicly known until 2005. The response of Germany
to discovering that some of its closest allies were listening
in to its people and its politicians was to ignore MEPs
who wanted to suspend trade talks between the US and
EU and put out feelers on becoming the sixth 'eye'. There
was little chance of that. Not only was the US historically
reluctant to extend the club beyond the key nations of
the so-called Anglosphere, Germany was historically
reluctant to take part in the more aggressive 'defence'
operations underpinned by the Five Eyes network, most
notably the Iraq invasion of 2003 which split the EU
down the middle. Britain's commitment to a common
EU defence and security programme was called into question across the continent. 'The UK's leaders take pride
in its partnership with the US and its membership of the

Five Eyes Pact. And, by most accounts, it does so with the substantial support of its citizens. This begs the question: how European is Britain?' wrote Juliane Mendelsohn, a lecturer in European law at Berlin's Free University, in *The European* magazine. Thorsten Benner, director of the Global Public Policy Institute (GPPi) in Berlin, added: 'There is no united Europe when it comes to surveillance. A chief enemy of privacy rights is part of the European Union: the government of the United Kingdom ... As the Snowden documents reveal, the NSA even pays the UK to operate as the European hub for surveillance.'

For many years after it joined the European club, Britain was firmly against extending the EU's remit to include a common defence policy. That was what NATO was for, the military alliance also based in Brussels that guarded Europe throughout the Cold War. In 1998, there was a sudden change of policy. Tony Blair, anxious to place Britain as 'one of the leading countries of Europe' but unable to join the euro because of Gordon Brown's opposition, made an announcement after talks at St Malo with Jacques Chirac, leader of the EU's other nuclear military power.

The European Union needs to be in a position to play its full role on the international stage ... This includes the responsibility of the European Council to decide on the progressive framing of a common defence policy in the framework of Common Foreign and Security Policy. The Union must have the capacity for autonomous action, backed up by credible military forces, the means to decide to use them and a readiness to do so, in order to respond to international crises. In order for the European Union to take decisions and approve military action where the Alliance [NATO] as a whole is not engaged, the Union must be given appropriate structures and a capacity for analysis of situations, sources of intelligence and a capability for relevant strategic planning, without unnecessary duplication.

The humanitarian, rescue and peace-keeping responsibilities of the Western European Union, a Cold War alliance dating back to 1954, were moved to the EU and a Common Security and Defence Policy developed. Blair agreed to the creation of eighteen joint EU battlegroups and, since 2007, two units of 1,500 troops are on constant standby. The units were seen as a prototype for the European Army that has long been the dream of integrationists, who believe that the EU cannot emerge as a true global power by the use of 'soft power' alone. Viviane Reding, Luxembourg's then member of the European Commission, tweeted in 2013 that: 'A European Army would be more efficient and would bring savings of between three and nine billion euros a year.' The December 2013 EU summit showed once again, however, that just as with intelligence security, the UK remained firmly against moving to the next level on European defence. Cameron objected to a plan for theEuropean Commission to have a stake in a 'European generation' of drones capable of flying for twenty-four hours, to be ready by 2020 for deployment at border crossing points and disaster areas. British diplomats purged the final communiqué of references to 'Europe's Armed Forces' and added clarification that defence policy should be left up to individual member states. Britain continued to resist calls for a permanent EU operational military headquarters, as it has done since this was first formally proposed in 2003 by France, Germany, Belgium and Luxembourg. 'What the EU does should be focused on practical action, facilitating what member states may want or choose to do together,' a Downing Street source told *The Times*. 'Take drones as an example. There can be no question of the Commission owning dual use military capabilities such as drones. Defence kit must be nationally owned and controlled and that should be clear to everyone.' A French call for an EU fund to help cover the costs of unilateral missions such as its armed intervention in Central African Republic was also shot down, this time by Germany.

Despite the obvious disagreements between Europe's major powers over defence and security coordination, there are those who believe that Britain has a lot to lose in this area by pulling out of the EU. Some analysts foresee a vacuum developing as the US tires of performing most of the heavy lifting for NATO to resolve problems in Europe's backyard while EU member states keep failing to step up to the mark. US impatience with Europe's continued weak military cooperation began with the wars triggered by the break-up of Yugoslavia. The Foreign Minister of Luxembourg, Jacques Poos, declared in 1991 that 'the hour of Europe has dawned' as he arrived to broker a peace treaty in Slovenia. In the wider context of the Balkans, however, he could not have been more wrong and Europe's disastrous inability to prevent or resolve the Bosnian and Kosovan wars in the 1990s left NATO with the responsibility of ending conflicts in which more than 100,000 died and two million were displaced. Fast-forward twenty years and Libya, another of Europe's neighbours, erupted into civil war. Once again there was EU political disagreement, with the spectacle at a Brussels summit in March 2011 of the EU High Representative for Foreign Affairs, Baroness Ashton, joining Germany in opposing the call from Britain and France for a no-fly zone to protect civilians. Thanks to a UN Security Council resolution just six days later in favour of a no-fly zone, the French and British began to enforce it the following week supported by the Americans in a mission soon taken over by NATO. If President Obama's 'pivot' towards Asia was not a clear enough sign that the US was beginning to move on from fighting Europe's battles, Robert Gates, the US Defense Secretary, gave notice in a speech in Brussels in 2011 of a 'dim if not dismal future' for NATO unless the Europeans started to pull their weight. 'For most of the Cold War US governments could justify defence investments and costly forward bases that made up roughly 50 per cent of all NATO military spending,' Gates said.

But some two decades after the collapse of the Berlin Wall, the US share of NATO defence spending has now risen to more than 75 per cent – at a time when politically painful budget and benefit cuts are being considered at home. The blunt reality is that there will be dwindling appetite and patience in the US Congress – and in the American body politic writ large – to expend increasingly precious funds on behalf of nations that are apparently unwilling to devote the necessary resources or make the necessary changes to be serious and capable partners in their own defence ... Indeed, if current trends in the decline of European defence capabilities are not halted and reversed, future US political leaders – those for whom the Cold War was *not* the formative experience that it was for me – may not consider the return on America's investment in NATO worth the cost.

With declining levels of national defence spending as a result of the financial crisis, the EU will have no choice but to develop its common defence and security system if its member states continue to neglect NATO and the US scales back its involvement. That means Britain, if it leaves the EU, could find itself left on the outside, or at best taking part as an associate rather than a full member. In an essay for Regent's University, Jolyon Howorth, Jean Monnet Professor of European Studies at Bath University, said:

Because the European defence and security project arises out of the movement of history's tectonic plates, Common Security and Defence Policy (CSDP) would have no alternative but to continue to develop, even

without the UK. By the same token, the UK, because it
is a significant defence player geographically situated in
Europe, would have no alternative but to continue to
have some sort of relationship with CSDP. This might
involve the negotiation of a special status for the UK
(similar to that of Turkey perhaps) within the European
security project. But whatever the precise nature of
such an arrangement, the UK would clearly henceforth
wield significantly less clout in CSDP than it has to
date ... The absence of the UK will undoubtedly lead
to ever closer security and defence cooperation between
France and Germany (however fraught with problems
programmatically and strategically), and, beyond that,
with the Weimar group (France, Germany and Poland)
supplemented by Italy and Spain. It would be very
difficult for France to find a justification for establishing
a privileged partnership with a 'post-Brexit' UK which
looked fixedly across the Atlantic rather than across
the Channel.

France, however, is fully aware that Brexit is a possibility
and nevertheless seems to have concluded that it stands
a better chance of remaining an important military actor
in a bilateral partnership with the UK than under the
EU's patchy CSDP. In 2013, after France intervened
(backed up by British non-combat support) in Mali
following a coup , Colonel Michel Goya, a teacher at the
Institut de Recherche Strategique de l'Ecole Militaire in
Paris, told the EUobserver website that, 'If you have to
react quickly to events, it is better to do it at a national

or bi-national level.' In other words, the EU was just too cumbersome to deliver a meaningful military response. France and the UK signed a Treaty on Defence and Security Co-operation in November 2010. The areas of cooperation include aircraft carriers, transport aircraft, nuclear submarines, military satellite technology, drones, expeditionary forces and eventually combat systems. The two countries are indisputably the EU's leading military powers, spending $115 billion on defence in 2014, more than Germany, Italy, the Netherlands, Poland and Spain put together. 'As shown from our joint operations in Libya and Mali, the UK and France are natural partners and have a key role to play in leading and shaping the defence and security of Europe,' a British Defence Ministry spokesman said in September 2012. The British and French army, navy and air force regularly train together and British officers serve full time on the French aircraft carrier, the *Charles de Gaulle*. They are on track to create a Combined Joint Expeditionary Force (CJEF) and are building a 'Future Combat Air System' due in 2030. The deepening military cooperation with France could be the foundation of a post-EU defence strategy for Britain, if one were needed.

EDUCATION, RESEARCH
AND SCIENCE

IN British academics won a disproportionately high number of grants from the European Research Council in 2015 (16.5 per cent) but British students take a disproportionately low number of placements at European universities on the Erasmus exchange scheme (5.4 per cent in 2012/13).

OUT The UK could still take part in the EU's research programme and Erasmus student exchange scheme, provided the other member states agreed and it paid to take part like Norway and Switzerland.

KEY STATS British-based researchers won €6.1 billion of the €50.5 billion available in the 2007–13 EU research programme (12 per cent), including €1.4 billion out of €7.5 billion of grants from the European Research Council.[45] There were 125,300 EU students at UK universities in 2013/14, 5.4 per cent of the total.[46]

After gaining his PhD in metal physics, Andre Geim spurned his native Russia to work in the US, UK and Netherlands before deciding that Britain was the best place to be based as an academic researcher. His initial notoriety came from discovering a magnetic technique with water which he demonstrated by levitating a frog. Then he published an academic paper in the name of his favourite hamster. As a professor at Manchester University, Geim and fellow Russian émigré Konstantin Novoselov discovered the ultra-thin material graphene in 2004 while funded by Britain's Engineering and Physical Sciences Research Council (EPSRC). Geim and Novoselov used a sophisticated form of sticky tape to strip graphite down to the atomic level. At just one molecule thick, graphene is a million times thinner than a sheet of paper but 200 times stronger than steel. 'We devote 10 per cent of our time to so-called "Friday evening" experiments,' said Novoselov. 'I just do all kinds of crazy things that probably won't pan out, but if they do ... This graphene business started as a Friday evening experiment.' Novoselov won an EU-funded grant of €1.78 million from the European Research Council in 2007 while Geim and his team picked up another £5 million from EPSRC in 2009 to work on the potential of graphene, which has been hailed as the wonder material of the twenty-first century, with the potential to replace silicon in computing among many other possible uses from 'wearable electronics' to stronger condoms. The pair was awarded the Nobel Prize for Physics in 2010. It was a big moment for the EPSRC but also for the European Research Council – Novoselov was the first Nobel laureate in its short history following its creation by the EU in 2007. The British government acted to try and ensure that graphene development stayed in the UK with grants of £21.5 million awarded in 2012 through the EPSRC to six universities, including Manchester where the National Graphene Institute was completed in 2015 with £38 million of government money and £23 million of EU regional development funding. Geim and Novoselov, who both hold joint citizenship, were

knighted in the New Year's Honours List 2012. The EU
went even further in 2013, announcing the 'Graphene
Flagship' deal – a ten-year research programme for 126
academic and industrial research groups in seventeen
European countries to be funded by €1 billion from the
EU budget. While Britain will clearly have to fight to
stay at the forefront of a material discovered at a British
university, the Graphene Flagship is one answer to those
who ask whether the EU ever spends taxpayers' cash on
forward-looking European innovation.

The EU's overall budget agreement for the seven-
year period from 2014 to 2020 saw the first real terms
cut in spending – by 3.7 per cent – following calls for
restraint led by the British government. Research was
one of the few policy areas to be handed an increase.
Spending will rise by 52.5 per cent to €77 billion from
€50.5 billion in 2007–13, with the European Research
Council receiving €13.1 billion of that, up from €7.5
billion. British universities and researchers do relatively
well in competition for EU grants with other countries
and are second only to their counterparts in Germany in
accessing EU research funding, winning €6.1 billion of
the 2007–13 budget. At around 12 per cent of the funds
available, this proportion was roughly equal to Britain's
contribution to the overall EU budget. It has become an
invaluable source of funding for several UK universities, accounting for at least 10 per cent of their research
income and helping to attract and keep top academics in
the UK. Cambridge ranked fourth among all participants
worldwide in the seven-year research programme from

2007 to 2013 with more than €370 million in grants, closely followed by Oxford with just under €370 million. The top ten also included University College London in seventh with €309 million and Imperial College London (ninth with €296 million). British businesses also received a slice of the cake with 2,800 firms sharing €800 million, with Rolls-Royce awarded €20 million in research cash. If Britain left the EU, it could pay to stay in the EU's research programme as non-EU member Switzerland did in the 2007–13 programme, signing an agreement to contribute €1.4 billion or 3 per cent of the budget. Its researchers received around €1.8 billion in funding. Swiss involvement had to be approved by other member states. But why would an independent UK pay to join an EU programme rather than simply commit the same level of funds to its own universities and companies? Most EU grants are given to consortia of researchers from several countries and only by full participation can a country lead one of these projects. It is possible to join in by invitation – and researchers from the US and around the world join consortia receiving EU funds – but the lead researcher must be based in a member state. Plus Britain would lose its role at the table when deciding on research strategy, such as the choice of graphene for one of two flagship projects chosen from twenty-three proposals.

At undergraduate level, growing numbers of universities across the EU are introducing courses in English to attract British students deterred by the steep rise in domestic course fees (except for Scottish students in Scotland) of up to £9,000 a year. Universities in Denmark and Sweden do not charge undergraduates for tuition while those in the Netherlands have a much lower fee, with the University of Maastricht staging a recruitment drive for British students for courses priced at €1,984 for the 2016/17 academic year. The numbers of EU students in British institutions had been rising quite sharply up until 2011/12, the last year before the full £9,000 fee came in, when the total reached 132,555. Since then the numbers have fallen back to 125,300 in 2013/14. Since Britain imports many more students from the EU than it exports, eurosceptics argue that there would be a large net income gain if UK institutions were able to charge full international fees. With classroom-based degrees generally costing one third more for non-EU students and medical courses three times as much, there could be a considerable windfall for UK universities in the event of British EU withdrawal – provided that even higher fees did not in turn put more EU students off. EU countries would also then apply international rates to British students, reducing their appeal, although in many cases they would still be cheaper – Maastricht University's tuition fee for non-EU students in 2016/17 is €7,500 a year for arts and €10,000 for science.

The EU's level playing field for undergraduate fees also means that EU students can access government-subsidised support from the Student Loan Company. But the recovery of these loans is causing growing concern. By the end of the 2013/14 financial year, the amount of money lent to European students was £686.3 million, with £263.9 million of this liable for repayment and £16.2 million classed as in arrears. The SLC announced in 2013 that it had hired private investigators to track down those evading payment in Europe. Loans for tuition costs would no longer have to be provided from the SLC to EU students if the UK withdrew from the Union.

One of the main pan-European higher education projects is the Bologna Process, founded in 1998 by the UK, France, Germany and Italy, to harmonise and integrate university processes and standards. This has been joined by forty-seven countries in the European Higher Education Area and, although EU member states lead the way, would remain open to the UK outside the EU. Cooperation and collaboration between scholars has been a feature of European higher education for centuries and will continue whether Britain is in or out of the EU. And despite fears to the contrary, a British departure from the EU need not bring an end to Erasmus, a popular scheme for student and staff placements in European universities. Erasmus provides grants for undergraduate placements of three to twelve months. Around 200,000 British students have been abroad on the Erasmus programme since it began in 1987, with 14,572 receiving a monthly allowance of up to €370 each from the EU in 2012/13. British universities receive around twice as many students as they send to Europe, a total of 27,182 in 2012/13. Erasmus was another of the few areas to receive a rise in the 2014–20 EU budget, going up by 40 per cent to €14.7 billion and extending the beneficiaries to include 'youth leaders, volunteers and young sportsmen'. This led some anti-EU MEPs to question why more cash should be spent on non-means-tested grants to university students while other initiatives are being cut. Stuart Agnew, a UKIP MEP, told the European Parliament:

> Erasmus is simply a glorified student exchange programme which we could do without the existence of the EU. UK universities have numerous exchange programmes all over the world without needing to be in a political union. Erasmus is not really about educational excellence, is it? It is to cynically use young people to further your political aims.

Mairead McGuinness, an Irish Fine Gael MEP, asked Agnew if he had 'any respect for young people and their ability to discern what is right and what is wrong and their ability as mature young people to live and to learn by sharing experience'. Agnew replied: 'I am not insulting youth at all. What really worries me is the way they are being used by the European Union to further its own objectives. Throw money at young people, tell them how wonderful the EU is and they will vote for it.' Several non-EU countries, however, including Turkey and Switzerland, have already joined Erasmus by paying a membership fee, so Britain could continue its involvement in the scheme should it leave the EU and provided that the member states accept an application to take part.

ENVIRONMENT, CLIMATE CHANGE AND ENERGY

IN Britain must reduce greenhouse gas emissions by 16 per cent by 2020 compared to 2005 under binding EU targets. Britain must reuse or recycle 50 per cent of household waste by 2020 under the Waste Framework Directive.

OUT Britain could scale back its ambitious renewable energy target and exempt manufacturers (but not exporters to the EU) from the Reach Directive on the safety of chemical compounds. A number of United Nations protocols demand strict environmental controls even if Britain found itself outside the EU.

KEY STATS The EU has adopted a binding target of 40 per cent lower greenhouse gas emissions than 1990 by 2030, while the UK has already set a national target of 50 per cent less by 2025. The UK is struggling to meet its EU target of 15 per cent of renewable energy by 2020. UK greenhouse gas emissions fell by 2.4 per cent from 2012 to 2013, and were below the cap set by the EU's Effort Sharing Decision for individual member states.[47]

Two small earthquakes hit the Lancashire coast in 2011 and signalled a new phase in the battle over a controversial technique for retrieving huge amounts of gas trapped deep under half the land mass of the UK. The tremors led to a temporary ban on the controversial technique of fracking – short for hydraulic fracturing – the practice of releasing gas from shale rock layers by blasting them with high pressure water and chemicals.

An independent report commissioned by the energy company Cuadrilla conceded it was 'highly probable' that the tremors were caused by its test drilling but added that earthquakes were 'unlikely to occur again' because of the 'unusual combination of geology' at the site. By December 2012, the government had lifted the national fracking ban but the European Commission was looking into the environmental implications of exploiting the potentially vast amount of gas lying underneath many EU countries. In Britain alone, reserves are said to be sufficient to supply the country with gas for at least fifty years, although experts caution that only a fraction could possibly be extracted. Still, after fracking transformed the energy debate in the United States by dramatically cutting both prices and greenhouse gas emissions, it is a huge temptation for politicians in Europe at a time of public disquiet over rising energy prices and an increasing reliance on gas and coal from Russia.

The EU already has an array of regulations to protect the environment from the potentially harmful side effects of fracking, such as ground water pollution controls and strict rules on greenhouse gas releases. So while France introduced a ban on the technique and Germany a moratorium, the UK government teamed up with Poland, the EU country with the largest gas reserves and fewest qualms about exploiting them, to put pressure on the bureaucrats in Brussels not to add to the legal constraints. 'It is essential the EU minimise the regulatory burdens and costs on industry and domestic bill payers by not creating uncertainty or introducing new legislation,' David Cameron wrote to José Manuel Barroso, then European Commission President, in December 2013. 'The industry in the UK has told us that new EU legislation would delay imminent investment.' In a leaked letter, Ivan Rogers, Britain's ambassador to the EU, warned that even if successful in avoiding the threat of legislation 'we will need a longer term strategy to manage the risks including ... an influencing strategy for the new European Parliament and Commission'. In January 2014, the European Commission decided against new laws on fracking although it said it would monitor drilling closely and review the situation. In a long-awaited announcement on its future environmental goals, the Commission also backed away from further tough national targets on renewable energy, recognising that some countries favoured nuclear energy and fracking as important parts of their energy mix. The British government's successful lobbying effort won an instant vote of confidence from French energy company Total which, shut out of its home market, announced investment of up to £30 million in test drilling in Lincolnshire. It also won admiring headlines, including the *Daily Mail*'s 'EU scraps targets forcing Britain to build wind farms: UK free to go nuclear and use fracking'. While the EU does not force wind farms on member states – it is their choice how to meet renewable targets – this reflected how Brussels has an important influence over environmental and energy choices. The question is whether the UK would be free and willing to make different choices following a vote to leave the Union.

Environmental legislation made in Brussels has long been a target of eurosceptics for criticism and potential repatriation to UK control. 'We need to examine whether the balance is right in so many areas where the European Union has legislated including on the environment, social affairs and crime. Nothing should be off the table,' Cameron said in his Bloomberg speech. In Open Europe's list of the most expensive EU regulations according to the government's own assessment studies, four of the top ten concern the environment, including the Climate and Energy Package of 2009 costing £3.36 billion a year and the Building and Approved Inspectors (Amendment) Regulations 2006 and the Energy Performance of Buildings (Certificates and Inspectors) (England and Wales) Regulations 2007 costing £1.5 billion a year. As seen in the Prosperity chapter, the government claimed a ludicrous level of potential benefits from the Climate and Energy Package when it was agreed in 2009. Instead, the costs have been huge. The package includes the Renewables Directive, the Emissions Trading Directive and the Directive on the Geological Storage of Carbon Dioxide – some of the most expensive and criticised of all the EU's attempts to give a global lead on environmental protection.

The Renewables Directive for the first time dictated to EU member states the make-up of their national energy mix. While not ordering any particular method, it brought in an EU target for 20 per cent of energy to come from renewable sources by 2020 across the member states, with Britain's share to rise from 1.3 per cent in 2005 to 15 per cent (the biggest leap of any country). UK ministers believed that incentives to make such a dramatic increase in wind, wave, biomass or solar power would flow from emissions trading, an experiment which Britain began in 2002 ahead of the EU's own Emissions Trading Scheme (ETS) at a time when the UK was keen to be seen as a world leader in green economics. It didn't work out as planned. The ETS has been a shambles because the EU handed out far too many permits. It reckoned without a fall in demand for energy caused by the recession which saw the price of permits crash from nearly €30 each in 2008 to a low of less than €3 in January 2013. Emissions actually rose by 1.9 per cent during the first phase of the EU trading scheme and by 5.8 per cent in the UK. From 2011 to 2012 EU emissions went up by 2.4 per cent and UK emissions by 3.2 per cent. The UK responded by introducing a floor price in its permits, set at £18.08 per tonne of CO_2 from to 2015 to 2020, going much further than the EU dared to go in adding costs to industry – and to consumers. While the EU moved in 2013 to delay issuing a large quantity of permits in an attempt to drive the prices back up, analysts predict it will still be years before they rise above the €20 level deemed necessary to prompt industry and utilities to make a fundamental shift to green energy. Two years of dramatic emission cuts in 2013 and 2014, attributed to a combination of climate policies, recession and an unseasonably warm 2014, mean that the EU has already overshot its target for 2020 of a 20 per cent reduction in greenhouse gases since 1990 by 3 percentage points. During the same period, the economy grew by 46 per cent, leading the EU to claim that climate protection and growth could go hand in hand.

Despite the success in meeting the EU's headline goal, Britain is struggling to meet its renewable energy target, with 7 per cent of energy consumption coming from renewable sources in 2014. The targets have failed to inspire sufficient capacity to replace that taken out under an EU measure to remove high-emitting facilities called the Large Combustion Plant Directive. This led to the closure of 11GW of UK generating capacity by the end of 2015. In 2013, the Fresh Start group of Conservative MPs warned that:

> The UK currently has around 97GW of generation capacity covering an estimated peak demand of 57.1GW. However, of this only 64.1GW of generation capacity is 'base load' or reliable for peak periods, this currently gives the UK a spare peak time capacity of 13 per cent. However, as a result of the removal of large plants from production the base load is predicted to fall to 46.8 GW. Unless measures are taken, this could leave the UK with very little or no peak time generation cover, potentially leading to blackouts.

The problem could be compounded by Britain's slow response to replacing its ageing nuclear energy capacity,

with the planned closure of 7GW of nuclear generation by 2020. The first new atomic plant commissioned by the UK government this century is not due
to come on line until at least 2023 at Hinkley Point
in Somerset. The contract with French provider EDF
was investigated by the European Commission's
competition directorate because of the government's
guarantee to pay a fixed amount for the nuclear energy
for thirty-five years, a price double the market rate in
2015. While the project was signed off by Brussels in
October 2014, EU member state Austria has lodged
an appeal at the European Court of Justice claiming
that it is subsidised illegally by under EU law. The plan
has thus been caught up in central European politics
– Austria was believed to have challenged the deal as
part of a wider strategy aimed at blocking the Czech
Republic and Hungary, its neighbours, from building new nuclear power stations. It represents another
potential stumbling block to the British government,
which is counting on Hinkley Point to provide 7 per
cent of the UK's electricity at full capacity. Meanwhile,
National Grid, the operator of Britain's energy pipes
and pylons, warned in October 2015 that the winter's
forecast capacity margin – the difference between
available supply and expected peak demand – was just
1.2 per cent before emergency additional measures,
making it the lowest since 2005–6.

It is tempting to blame the EU for causing Britain's
potential energy crunch by a mixture of ambitious greenhouse gas targets, the forced closure of coal-fired power

stations and a failed investment strategy due partly to the problems of the Emissions Trading Scheme. But the UK has actually been running ahead of Brussels on most of these environmentally inspired measures. Britain's transition to low-carbon energy began in 2000 with a Royal Commission on Environmental Pollution that recommended a cut in emissions by 60 per cent below 1990 levels by 2050. Then Ed Miliband, as Energy and Climate Change Secretary, announced that the 2008 Climate Change Act would require the government to cut emissions by 80 per cent by 2050 in the toughest target set by any country in the world. In May 2011, Chris Huhne, then Energy and Climate Secretary, committed the UK to making 50 per cent emissions cuts by 2025. Successive British governments have imposed strict environmental targets on themselves.

Outside the EU, Britain could revise its renewable energy target of 15 per cent by 2020, although it was content to sign up to this under the Labour government in 2009. It could have repealed the regulations that implemented the Large Combustion Plant Directive but a policy u-turn back to higher emissions from coal-fired power stations would face stiff opposition on environmental grounds – even with cheap coal becoming available from the US as it steps up its gas production from fracking. And the UK could accelerate its own use of the controversial gas extraction technique, although it has been hampered far more by earthquakes in Lancashire than interference from Brussels. EU directives on water and air pollution will act as safeguards when fracking does begin in earnest and are unlikely to be repealed by an independent UK outside the EU.

One expensive directive that has hit industry hard is the Registration, Evaluation, Authorisation and Restriction of Chemicals (Reach) law of 2009 which requires companies to test and register with a new European Chemicals Agency every chemical compound used in their processes, above the level of one tonne per year. Although companies can share information, compliance costs have been estimated at €5 billion across the EU with a million more tests on animals required. Supporters say that it will more than pay for itself in savings in healthcare and environment costs. An independent UK could exempt manufacturers but not exporters of the onerous requirements. Reach's companion measure, the Classification, Labelling and Packaging (CLP) Regulation, which seeks to harmonise the way hazardous materials are classified and labelled, could not be similarly avoided, however, as it effectively implements the UN's Global Harmonized System for classifying hazardous substances. Similarly, many other EU environmental measures stem from international bodies. These include several important UN agreements such as the Gothenburg Protocol of 1999 setting limits for air pollutants; the Aarhus Convention of 2001 on public rights to environmental data; and the Kiev Protocol of 2010 on cross-border consultation on major projects with environmental impacts. Moreover there are signs of a slowdown in the EU's rush to be best in class for global environment lessons. The EU's new target of 40 per cent lower emissions by 2030 is far less ambitious than the target agreed by the British coalition government of 50 per cent by 2025. And following the announcement of a move from an overall 20 per cent EU renewable energy target by 2020 to 27 per cent by 2030, without binding individual country goals, environmental campaigners accused the European Commission of bowing to national pressure. 'The previously far-sighted and ambitious European Commission is a shadow of its former self, hiding behind the UK and other backward-looking member states and lobbies,' said Thomas Becker, CEO of the European Wind Energy Association. 'By effectively advocating repatriation of energy policy to member states, President Barroso appears to have forgotten his previous calls for "more European integration" on energy policy.' This was music to the ears of those campaigning for a return of environmental controls from Brussels and a sign that powers could occasionally flow from the EU back to national capitals.

EMPLOYMENT AND
SOCIAL LAW

IN Employee protections brought in by the EU include four weeks' minimum paid annual leave, fourteen weeks' minimum maternity leave and four further months of possible childcare leave, equal treatment for agency workers and limits to working hours.

OUT Britain would be able to scrap expensive EU laws like the Working Time Directive but only if it left the Single Market. Small and medium-sized businesses could be exempted from expensive employee protections like equal treatment for agency workers.

KEY STATS The 100 most costly EU regulations are estimated to cost the UK economy £27.4 billion per year with the Working Time Directive alone said to cost £4.1 billion a year.[48]

In its founding treaty dating back to 1957, the fore-runner of the European Union declared that one of its key aims was to 'promote improved working conditions and an improved standard of living for workers, so as to make possible their harmonisation' among the member states. Jacques Delors, the former French finance minister who was President of the European Commission from 1985 to 1994, made 'Social Europe' one of his top priorities. Delors, a Socialist who became the great nemesis of Britain's Conservative Prime

Minister Margaret Thatcher, believed that the opening up of the Single Market should go hand-in-hand with the protection of workers' rights. He reasoned that unfettered competition could lead companies to relocate to cheaper areas or drive them to cut costs ruthlessly, leading to worsening workplace conditions, insecurity and job losses. 'The creation of a vast economic area, based on market and business cooperation, is inconceivable – I would say unattainable – without some harmonisation of social legislation. Our ultimate aim must be the creation of a European Social Area,' Delors said in 1986. The British government refused to sign up. The clash of ideologies helped to create the impression that a European superstate was being built by an alternative powerbase in Brussels. As mentioned in the Sovereignty chapter, Britain felt that the Working Time Directive and its provision for a maximum working week of forty-eight hours was brought in by the back door and that Britain was being bounced into a new era of involuntary European integration. 'The UK strongly opposes any attempt to tell people that they can no longer work the hours they want,' said David Hunt, the Employment Secretary.

The Working Time Directive would go on to have a big impact on British life and become emblematic of the 'red tape' from Brussels, even though the government has secured the possibility for individuals to opt out of its 48-hour working week. Nowhere was the impact of this directive more acutely felt than in the National Health Service, where the long hours culture of junior doctors in hospitals was already being tackled by a government 'New Deal' to bring in a 56-hour maximum working week. The Working Time Directive also provides for four weeks' paid holiday from work, a minimum rest period of eleven consecutive hours in every twenty-four and a minimum uninterrupted rest period of twenty-four hours every seven days. Its provisions were advanced by several rulings from the European Court of Justice, adding on-call time to working hours calculations even when the worker was having a sleep. As the Royal College of Physicians observed in a briefing paper in 2012, the Working Time Directive (WTD) played havoc with NHS training, rotas and consultant care. 'The training time for junior doctors with senior consultants has been reduced,' the Royal College wrote.

Application of WTD and the New Deal has resulted in more rota gaps, which are often left to junior doctors to fill. Therefore many trainee doctors are working much of their time at night and unsupervised, missing out on crucial learning opportunities with more senior colleagues. This may result in the need for prolongation of training for some individuals. This has significant potential implications for future patient care ... Similarly, there is insufficient out of hours consultant cover. This is particularly problematic for small district general hospitals providing acute services. A survey by the RCP in October 2010 found that only 3 per cent of hospitals provided weekend cover from consultant physicians specialising in acute medicine for nine to twelve hours and none for over twelve hours.

The bulk of the annual NHS bill for locum doctors of £1 billion is for cover required due to the Working Time Directive and the total cost of the directive to the economy is estimated by Open Europe at £4.1 billion a year.

An estimated three million workers in Britain make use of the opt-out to work longer than forty-eight hours a week some or all of the time, from the hospitality industry to night porters, construction workers and contract labourers. The European Commission is keen to end the possibility of the individual opt-out but could only do so if a qualified majority of member states backed this in the European Council. So far, Britain is leading a blocking alliance – something it would not be able to do if it left the EU. If a post-referendum Britain joined the EEA, it would still have to apply the directive because it is deemed to be part of the Single Market. So if the European Commission got its way, a post-Brexit Britain in the EEA would also have to implement the 48-hour week with no opt-outs. In one example of the directive's far-reaching implications, Open Europe quoted David Dalziel, secretary of the Chief Fire Officers Association in Scotland, saying:

The potential loss of the individual opt-out in the UK would have catastrophic effects. Ninety-one per cent of the UK landmass is protected by firefighters on the retained duty system. These men and women crew two out of every three fire stations in the country. They hold other jobs in their local communities and also provide around 120 hours availability every week of the year to deliver a local fire and rescue service. Any adverse impact on that would expose this country to an unacceptable level of risk.

Labour and the Liberal Democrats have both spoken out against the way that the EU seeks to regulate employment through the Working Time Directive. But worker protections portrayed as bureaucratic and expensive by British business and politicians are viewed quite differently by the trade unions. In 2009, Brendan Barber, then General Secretary of the Trades Union Congress, said:

Long hours cause stress, illness and lower productivity. And when many employers are moving to short-time working, the need for an opt-out of the 48-hour week is even more out of date. The UK government still needs to tighten the law on working time, otherwise the EU could take it to court in order to protect UK workers from abuse of the 48-hour week.

Speaking at a TUC debate which voted overwhelmingly to end the British opt-out from the Working Time Directive, Tony Woodley, then joint leader of Britain's biggest union Unite, said: 'People don't want long hours. They work long hours because it is the only way to make ends meet. People should work to live – not live to work.' In 2013, Frances O'Grady, who replaced Barber as TUC General Secretary, said: 'Paid holidays

and other workplace rights are some of the best arguments for EU membership. Leaving the EU would be
disastrous for jobs and investment.'

After the Working Time Directive, the next most expensive directive on working conditions is thought to be the
Temporary Agency Workers Directive of 2008 which
brought extra annual costs estimated at £2 billion, according to Open Europe in 2013. The directive insists that
general working conditions for agency workers should be
the same as if they were recruited directly to the same
job by the same organisation. The government negotiated
with the Confederation of British Industry (CBI) and the
TUC for this requirement to come into effect once an
agency worker has completed twelve continuous calendar
weeks in the same role, at the same organisation. Like all
EU directives, it had to be brought in via UK law and was
implemented by the Agency Workers Regulations 2010.
The government's impact assessment estimated that
around 40 per cent of agency workers, around 520,000,
would be covered by the principle of equal treatment. It
also forecast that about 65,000 agency workers could
have their postings cut short to prevent them meeting the
twelve-week qualifying period for equal treatment. In a
survey of 200 medium-sized and large UK organisations
in 2011, one third of respondents said that they would
consider ending an agency workers' job before they had
served twelve weeks, in order to avoid the increased costs
of equal treatment.

There are dozens of other EU social and employment
laws, many concerned with technical aspects of health

and safety, which the UK would wish to preserve even if it withdrew from Brussels. Ordinary workers have undoubtedly benefited, notably on maternity and paternity leave. The Pregnant Workers' Directive of 1992 established the basic right of a working mother to fourteen weeks off to give birth, as well as time off with protection from dismissal for ante-natal examinations. The Parental Leave Directive of 1996 brought a new right, included in the Employment Relations Act 1999, for every parent to take thirteen weeks unpaid leave to care for each child (in addition to maternity leave) before the child turns five years old. This was the kind of social provision from Brussels that Conservative governments had blocked, in this case since it was first proposed by the European Commission in 1983. The Parental Leave Directive of 1996 was then repealed by the EU in 2010 and replaced with a more far-reaching provision, enacted into British law in 2013 by Statutory Instrument No. 283, to extend unpaid parental leave from thirteen to eighteen weeks.

The Working Time Directive appeared to be one of the Brussels laws that David Cameron originally had in his sights for renegotiation before the referendum on membership. In his 2012 speech to the Davos conference, he said:

In spite of the economic challenge, we are still doing things to make life even harder. In the name of social protection, the EU has promoted unnecessary measures that impose burdens on businesses and governments, and can destroy jobs. The Agency Workers Directive, the

Pregnant Workers Directive, the Working Time Directive. The list goes on and on.

Cameron was urged by the Fresh Start group to take back the powers conceded in 1997 when Tony Blair reversed John Major's position and agreed to sign up to the Social Chapter, giving the EU control over social and employment law. Such a return of powers to the national level over the whole field of employment and social legislation would require a change to the EU's treaties, something that requires unanimous agreement by all twenty-eight member states.

In his Bloomberg speech, Cameron again suggested that he wanted to try and take back powers over employment laws:

> We cannot harmonise everything. For example, it is neither right nor necessary to claim that the integrity of the single market or full membership of the European Union requires the working hours of British hospital doctors to be set in Brussels irrespective of the views of British parliamentarians and practitioners.

Other EU leaders had a different view – they believe that any such return of powers will unpick the necessary worker protections which go hand-in-hand with competition in the Single Market and lead to an unravelling of the entire EU project. Didier Reynders, the Belgian foreign minister, told Cameron in October 2013 that he wished to see the UK remain part of the EU but this could not mean 'à la carte' membership, echoing the warning to Britain in May 2012 from President Hollande of France, that 'Europe is not a cash till and less still a self-service restaurant'. In the face of stiff opposition from several European countries, Cameron abandoned any attempt to reverse or repatriate any EU employment and social laws ahead of the referendum. Instead, as part of his draft renegotiation deal, Cameron secured a commitment from the European Commission to 'establish a mechanism to review the body of existing EU legislation for its compliance with the principle of subsidiarity and proportionality'. This followed on from the regulatory fitness and performance programme, known as Refit, introduced by the Commission in 2015 to cut red tape, which promised 'specific targets ... for reducing the burden on business, particularly in the most onerous areas for companies, in particular small and medium-size enterprises'.

FARMING

IN British farmers belong to the same regime of subsidies and production standards as their European competitors, with UK ministers taking part in discussions to set the rules. Farmers are protected from global competition by common EU tariffs on imports.

OUT Britain would stop paying subsidies to European farmers while being free to modernise support payments to its own farmers and drop tariffs on imports to benefit consumers.

KEY STATS The Common Agricultural Policy took 39.6 per cent of EU spending, or €56 billion, in 2015. Nearly 200,000 British farmers shared £3.1 billion in 2015 from the EU, while £5.1 billion went to farming from the UK budget contribution, a net British subsidy to European farmers of £2 billion, or £5.5 million a day.[49]

At number nine on the 2015 *Sunday Times* Rich List with an estimated fortune of £8.56 billion, the 6th Duke of Westminster owed his great wealth to inherited land in some of the country's most desirable postcodes, including Mayfair and Belgravia in central London. His bank account is also boosted by a nice annual cheque from the European Union. His Grace's rural holdings received £748,716 through the Common Agricultural Policy (CAP) in 2011, according to information obtained from the Department for Environment, Food and Rural Affairs under Freedom of Information laws. He was not the only wealthy landowner helped by the taxpayer under the EU's oldest and most expensive system of subsidies. The Earl of Plymouth received £675,085, the Duke of Buccleuch £260,273, the Duke of Devonshire £251,729 and the Duke of Atholl £231,188. Brussels did not overlook the Windsor family. The Queen was given £415,817 for the Royal Farms and £314,811 for the Duchy of Lancaster, while Prince Charles was paid £127,868 for the Duchy of Cornwall.[50] An outcry over the amount of EU funds given to the extremely wealthy led to an attempt to limit annual payments under the CAP to €300,000 per owner. At the forefront of those opposing this move was the UK government, arguing that it would unfairly penalise British farmers for creating efficient, larger farms in contrast with the relatively uncompetitive smallholdings common in, say, France. 'The European Commission has this culture that small farms is how you do farming. We come from a completely different farming culture,' a British official said. Britain would have 330 farms losing money because of the proposed limit; France just thirty. In the end, the reform – like so many previous attempts to modernise the CAP – was watered down. In a compromise agreement, national governments must deduct at least 5 per cent from farm payments of more than €150,000 a year and can cut up to 100 per cent of the money above that level from 2015. The British government decided not to make any reductions to payments to wealthy landowners beyond the minimum 5 per cent. MPs on the Commons Select Committee for Environment, Food and Rural Affairs called for a higher rate of reduction for farms receiving more than €300,000 a year. But Owen Paterson, the Secretary of State, explained that, 'I do not want to see our successful farmers spending hours and hours with expensive solicitors artificially carving up their holdings to avoid an arbitrary diktat on the size of their holding.' In other words, there was no point trying to reduce subsidies for rich landowners because they would only find a way to keep them. Between them, Brussels and Westminster seem incapable of finding a fairer way of funding farming.

Financial support for farmers has been a core European activity since the Common Agricultural Policy started in 1962. It was the price France demanded in return for agreeing to free trade in industrial goods. After the short-ages and rationing of the post-war years, the aim was to ensure food security for Europe as well as to maintain the traditional farming practices which are so important for the rural economy, the landscape and the environment. Although the cost of the CAP reached 94 per cent of the EU budget in 1970, reform and the growing impor-tance of regional funding slowly reduced that amount to 39.6 per cent by 2015, although it remains way out of kilter for a sector which employs 5 per cent of Europeans and contributes 1.7 per cent to the EU economy – and just 0.7 per cent in the UK. Subsidies have been de-coupled from production, avoiding the 'butter mountains' and 'wine lakes' of the 1980s when farmers produced simply to earn subsidy rather than for the market. Most of the support money is now given out based on the size of the farm, benefiting the biggest landowners, although there are increasing efforts to link payments to environmental targets. Other new rules require farms of a certain size to grow at least three different crops, while an 'active farmer' test will identify land being used as an airfield or golf course which received payments in the past. With an average age of sixty for hill farmers in Britain and a struggle generally to attract young people to work on the land, there will also be cash incentives to the under-forties who take on farms.

Despite the latest tweaks to the Common Agricultural Policy, the main British political parties remain fundamentally opposed to the unconditional way the EU hands out most of its farm funding. Both Labour and the Conservatives wanted to phase out direct payments by 2020 but were continually blocked by other countries. Britain has long argued for more open world trade, which would allow poorer countries easier access to sell their produce to Europe and stop subsidised European farmers distorting markets in other countries with artificially cheaper goods that make it harder for local farmers to make a living. As explained in the Prosperity chapter, the average British household pays an annual premium of €324 to subsidise farmers. The consumer would therefore seem to have much to gain from leaving the EU and its CAP but the farmer would have much to lose.

A unilateral decision to pull out of the EU would not end the need to hand public money to farmers to keep some of them afloat, however, especially given the precarious and volatile nature of world food prices, and the subsidies received by competitors in other countries. In fact, one reason why the Norwegians and the Swiss voted not to join the EU was because of pressure from their farmers to keep even more generous subsidies. The average EU payment across all types of farm in the UK was £22,400 in 2014–15. Livestock grazing farmers in hill farms were the poorest paid and most supported, with an annual average income of £14,600 after costs, including average support worth £15,500 per farm from the CAP.[51] Non-EU Norway is not in the CAP and provides its farmers with 60 per cent of their average income, while Switzerland gives a hand-out of 55 per cent of average farm earnings, according to the OECD. Farmers in the EU received an average of 19 per cent of their income from Brussels in 2012–14, close to the OECD average of 18 per cent, but higher than the 10 per cent in Russia, 10 per cent in the US and 2 per cent in Australia.

The UKIP response is attractive – simply create a British system of farm payments to provide domestic farmers with the same level of support as the EU, drop the bureaucratic requirements, limit the annual maximum payout and pocket the difference from the UK's net subsidy to continental competitors of at least £2 billion a year. Farmers are a little more cautious. 'In the past, all the main political parties have said they want to phase out subsidies by 2020. I think it is more likely if a system of subsidy is going to be maintained, it will be less than we get now with the CAP,' Lucia Zitti, an economist with the National Farmers' Union, told Reuters in January 2016. The union's members were 'quite split', she added. 'They want to understand more about the implications of a possible Brexit and also hear how the EU can work better for farmers.' Charlie Flindt, a farmer from Hampshire, told Reuters that even simple jobs like putting up a fence to protect walkers from cattle involved annoying bureaucracy. 'You cannot simply put in a fence any more, and the hoops we have to jump through to get our European Union subsidies just pile up year and year. Most of us went into this job to get away from paperwork.' Flindt, who has an arable farm with a few sheep and cattle, said he could not believe a British-based system, outside the EU, would be 'as Kafkaesque as it is at the moment'. If Britain left the EU, the government could end the current requirements to link around one third of the farm subsidy to environ-mental measures, which would be welcomed by many farmers. According to the eurosceptic former farming and environment minister Owen Paterson, it could also speed up approval times for new technologies such as genetically modified crops and new crop protection chemicals. 'British agriculture, brimming with potential, is held back by prejudice against advanced technology and science,' Paterson said at the 2016 Oxford Farming Conference. 'The obstinate refusal to adopt advanced technology means Europe has become the museum of world farming.' The Scottish government is strongly opposed to GM crops, there is also a lot of resistance in Wales, and Northern Ireland announced a complete ban in September 2015. These reservations among the home nations show that leaving the EU would not make it politically easier to introduce GM technology, although it would end the requirement to seek approval from the European Food Safety Authority.

Peter Kendall, former President of the National Farmers' Union, in an article for Regent's University in 2013, said:

> British farmers are, by and large, more favourable to the European Union than the generality of the British public. Eurosceptics often ascribe this, rather cynically, to the fact that they are subsidised by the EU. An historical reminder is required here. The reason that there is a Common Agricultural Policy is that, in order to create a common market in farm goods, it was necessary to harmonise the various national agricultural policies to avoid trade distortions, real or perceived. For the National Farmers' Union, it is not the quantity of support that is important, it is equality of treatment with our competitors. Indeed, the NFU has stated that it would be prepared to see support for farmers phased out, provided this happened equally across the European Union. Concerns about the distortions of competition which would occur if levels of support were to be very different are real, and of course would be particularly acute if they occurred on either side of a land border – say Ulster and the Republic of Ireland, or an independent Scotland inside the EU and England outside.

However, the National Farmers' Union decided not to take an official position on whether to remain or leave in the EU referendum ahead of the results of Cameron's renegotiation. 'At this stage we simply can't,' it said in a statement. 'It's impossible to measure the impact of being outside the EU since we do not know the relationship the UK would have with the EU nor the conditions under which our farmers would be expected to operate if we left.' Instead it produced a report on the farming industry's relationship with the EU, pointing out that Britain imports 'nearly twice as many agri-food products from other EU countries than we export', although UK exports remained 'significant' at £12.8 million in 2014. For some sectors, the EU is 'critical', it said. The NFU also stressed the importance of foreign labour for British agriculture, saying: 'Any restriction on our members' ability to recruit non-UK-born workers would have a negative impact on their businesses.' Thirty-eight per cent of all lamb produced in the UK is exported to the EU, the NFU added, with France alone purchasing more than £200 million in 2014. If Britain was to move outside the Single Market, there is a risk that Brussels could apply its normal tariff of almost 40 per cent on foreign lamb imports. That would allow French farmers with their higher production costs a way back into the market. In his 2013 article, Kendall was wary of those who say that, because the UK has a trade deficit with the EU (it imports from Europe more than it exports), it would be in the EU's interests not to impose tariffs or other costs on British goods and risk a tit-for-tat trade war. Kendall continued:

The argument is frequently made that because we are net importers from the EU, it would not be in the interest of other members of the EU to see barriers to trade erected between the UK and the EU. From an agricultural point of view, at least, this is dubious. If the UK wishes to lower its tariff barriers with the rest of the world it would not, under WTO rules, be able to apply higher barriers to the EU. So the ability of the EU to export to the UK would be protected; the reverse would not apply.

The concerns of farmers at their fate if Britain left the EU are understandable. They could benefit like all businesses from a reduction in red tape and form-filling, and avoid some aggravating measures such as the EU requirement for electronic tagging of sheep, brought in to track animals following the foot and mouth outbreak, which is expensive to implement. 'The process of legislating a very detailed common policy by twenty-eight governments in co-decision with the European Parliament is extremely cumbersome and often easily open to criticism and even ridicule,' said Kendall.

The proposition that outside the EU we could devise a policy which was simpler, cleaner, less bureaucratic and more relevant is one that is bound to appear attractive. But that could also lead to negative developments as far as the farming community is concerned, if UK government support for the sector failed to deliver comparable outcomes for British farmers.

FISHING

IN Britain manages its territorial waters extending twelve miles from its coast but the EU decides fishing quotas and negotiates access to neighbouring zones. Pushed by Britain, the EU agreed radical reforms in 2013 to the failed Common Fisheries Policy to phase out the vast amount of discarded fish.

OUT Britain regains sovereignty over its Exclusive Economic Zone extending 200 miles from its coast and can implement fish preservation measures to revive over-fished stocks. It would have to negotiate access rights to waters controlled by the EU, Norway, Iceland and Faroes.

KEY STATS 48 per cent of Atlantic stocks and 93 per cent of Mediterranean stocks were classified as over-fished in 2015; the EU is phasing in a 'landing obligation' from 2015 to 2019 after an outcry over the million tonnes of mainly dead fish thrown back every year; €2.73 billion was spent by the EU to scrap vessels between 1994 and 2013 and yet over-capacity increased by 3 per cent a year.[52]

From the deck of the Scottish trawler *Seagull*, the true obscenity of the EU's disastrous Common Fisheries Policy (CFP) was clear to see. Basket after basket of prime cod were thrown back dead into the North Sea off the Shetlands – not because there was anything wrong with them, but because the fishermen had already exceeded their EU quota for catching one of Britain's favourite fish. The *Seagull* was only allowed to bring back monkfish, megrim and ling. So all other types of dead or dying fish that did not meet strict EU criteria but had been captured in the nets as 'by-catch', such as the edible but unglamorous coley, were also dumped back into the sea. This was a scene from the hidden devastation of the CFP as revealed in 2011 by the celebrity chef Hugh Fearnley-Whittingstall in his TV series *Fish Fight*. 'I can't put a sign on the nets saying, "No cod today, please." I hate discarding fish,' said Gary Much, the skipper of the 400-tonne trawler. 'If we could land all the fish we catch, we could go to sea for half as many days, use half the fuel and no fish would be wasted. It is madness.' The EU estimated that one million tonnes of edible fish was simply thrown back every year by European fishermen. That was enough to supply all of Britain's fish and chip shops for a decade. Often the fishermen had caught less favoured fish and needed to make room on their boat or save their ice for more valuable ones. 'The crazy irony is that the quota system is meant to conserve fish stocks, particularly cod. But it seems obvious to me you cannot conserve fish by throwing a million tonnes of them back in the sea, dead,' said Fearnley-Whittingstall. Clearly the situation, which existed for thirty years, was ripe for reform but it took a campaign by a celebrity chef and a petition signed by 870,000 people to bring about change. The British government led the push for reform. 'It is indefensible. Imagine if farmers threw away half their lambs, cattle and pigs. There would be rioting in the streets,' said Richard Benyon, the fisheries minister. 'The current CFP has failed. It has not given us healthy fish stocks and it has not delivered a sustainable living for our fishing industry. Only genuine fundamental reform of this broken policy can turn around these failures.' The huge waste of discards seemed to sum up everything that was wrong with the EU's handling of its fisheries, with once plentiful species such as cod, bluefin tuna and anchovy fished almost to extinction in some areas as politicians overruled scientific advice when setting catch levels year in, year out. Fishing seemed one policy area where Britain would make a much better job of managing its own sovereign territory if it left the EU.

Almost three years on from the launch of the *Fish Fight* campaign, the unthinkable happened. In December 2013, the European Parliament voted in favour of a ban on discards of fish at sea following months of hard negotiations between ministers from the EU's fishing nations. Discards are being phased out between 2015 and 2019 depending on species and region. Only species that are known to have a good survival rate after being caught can be thrown back, all others must be landed. Young fish too small for normal sale will go as animal feed for a nominal price that does not encourage their capture, while fishermen who exceed their annual quota will have to buy spare allowances from their countrymen or have quotas reduced the following year. Among measures to monitor the discard ban, CCTV is being installed on some boats. This was not all – the discard ban was accompanied by a wider reform to ensure that scientific advice governs catching limits for each species known as Maximum Sustainable Yields, while more power was devolved to national authorities to allocate quotas and manage fleets in a process called regionalisation. The impressive reform package seemed to show that terrible EU policies could be changed, even if this one took three decades. 'We've got what we asked for,' said Fearnley-Whittingstall on his blog.

> Where the (crazy) old CFP said that fishermen had to discard fish that they didn't have quota for, the new CFP says that this is wasteful and every effort must go towards ending discards. It's a huge result for people power and sustainable policy-making. Massive thanks go out to everyone who signed up and got active, and to the politicians, fishermen, campaigners and scientists who have supported this cause.

There are warnings that the discard ban will not by itself save Europe's fishing industry and there are still tough decisions to be made on reducing the fleet capacity. But the story of the Common Fisheries Policy might yet have a happy ending. It has long been one of the most obvious EU powers that could be returned to national level, however, and the surprisingly enlightened reforms of 2013 have not changed the minds of some of those who cannot forgive the many years of inept top-down management from Brussels. The policy was originally dreamed up by the founding six member states when it became clear that the fishing nations of Ireland, Denmark and the UK were planning to join in 1973. The entry of Spain and Portugal in 1986 added vast extra territory and fleets, leading to chronic overcapacity which the EU did little to control. Politicians from the member states were put in charge of the final say on annual catch levels in a ritual Christmas showdown in Brussels which saw scientific advice routinely ignored. As a result of over-fishing, the annual catch of British fishermen is just one-tenth of what it was a century ago. In 2008, when 93 per cent of cod were caught before reaching the maturity required to breed, the EU set an even higher catch quota for the following year. Campaign groups still want a big cut in the EU fleet but the EU has already spent €2.73 billion on a scheme to 'buy out' fishermen and scrap their licences which actually saw fishing capacity rise because of the greater efficiency of the latest vessels, equipment and technology.

Britain's Exclusive Economic Zone, which covers all the sea and everything in it up to a distance of 200 nautical miles from its coast, is the largest of any EU country with the greatest range of fish species. The UK also has the second largest fisheries tonnage of the EU and the second largest processing industry. Regaining sovereignty over the sea, which is only possible by leaving the EU, would mean that Britain can close areas when stocks need time to regenerate and it can legally ban vessels from other nations. However, a block on one country's fishermen could lead to reciprocal measures on British fishermen in return and many of the most important fish, such as cod, herring, mackerel, plaice and whiting, migrate between several territorial areas during the course of their lives. As one fisherman's representative put it, crab and scallops are fairly sedentary but everything with a tail requires joint management with other jurisdictions. This mobility led to long-running 'mackerel wars' between the EU (acting mainly on behalf of Scottish fishermen in the north-east Atlantic), Iceland and the Faroes, as the species migrated into the northern nations' waters in greater numbers, possibly due to sea warming. The EU reached an agreement in 2014, which has been criticised by Scotland for handing too much of the mackerel quota to the Faroes. Catching limits agreed in 2015 by the EU included 15 per cent reductions for mackerel to help conserve stocks – an outcome welcomed in Scotland because it was a lower reduction than originally discussed. 'The UK would clearly have a critical interest in ensuring that appropriate conservation policies were applied to those "straddling" stocks in order to avoid their being damaged by overfishing by other countries' vessels,' said Andy Lebrecht, the former UK deputy permanent representative in Brussels in an essay for Regent's University in 2013.

The only way to achieve this would be to enter into formal fisheries agreements with the EU and with Norway to deliver 'joint management', along the lines of the current EU–Norway agreement for the North Sea. Indeed, article 63 of the UN Conference of the Law of the Sea requires coastal states to do precisely this. Any negotiated joint management agreements would of necessity have to specify the share out of the stocks concerned. It is moreover all but certain that the other member states (and Norway) would insist on their current 'relative stability' shares of the Total Allowable Catches concerned and access to the UK's Exclusive Economic Zone (as now) as part of any such agreement. Given that the 'relative stability' settlement has endured for thirty years and was itself based on historic fishing patterns, it is difficult to see how the UK could articulate a convincing argument for any alternative allocation of fishing rights.

Shared fishing stocks are a biological reality of the seas and a failure to agree joint management plans with neighbouring authorities such as Norway, Iceland and the EU could result in a free-for-all, which would inevitably lead to overfishing. Exports to Europe could also become subject to the EU's Common External Tariff depending on the trade deal that Britain ends up negotiating with Brussels after leaving.

Until the recent EU reforms, the case for Britain claiming back its historic fishing grounds was overwhelming. After many years of failure, the Common Fisheries Policy may have been saved, in no small part thanks to the efforts of British fishermen and ministers, from a system that had become politicised and detached from science, best practice and local needs. Barry Deas, of the National Federation of Fishermen's Organisations, said:

> Only time will tell if regionalisation will become an effective counterweight to central control in Brussels, which has been really the reason why the Common Fisheries Policy has been so ineffectual on the conservation front. The model of command and control is thoroughly discredited and a move towards decentralisation is

recognised as necessary to lay the foundations of a more effective policy.

As for the move to end discards, he added:

> What it will mean in practice, everybody including the scientists and the industry are scratching their heads over implementing it successfully on the ground. This is certainly going to be destabilising because in many ways it turns things on its head – for example, one of the fisheries with a high level of discards is plaice, but plaice stocks are doing very well despite the high level of discards and one of the reasons is that quite a high proportion of them survive, maybe 60 per cent, when you put them back. If you now are obliged to take them ashore, dead, they are not going to be contributing to the biomass. Everybody wants to reduce discards but it is just not as straightforward as some people think.

Norway kept control over its fisheries after deciding not to join the EU in 1973 and has had its own discard ban since 1987. It has negotiated access for its fishermen to EU waters and vice versa, with the EU making Norway's access to the Single Market conditional upon allowing European vessels to fish in Norwegian waters. It is far too soon to tell if the EU's reorganised Common Fisheries Policy will provide the modernised and responsible fishing industry that consumers want. But it makes the decision to leave the EU based on fishing concerns a little less clear-cut than it has been for decades.

JUSTICE

IN Britain exercised its right to opt out of all 133 EU justice policies agreed before the Lisbon Treaty of 2009 and is opting back into thirty-five of them, including the European Arrest Warrant (EAW) and the police cooperation agency Europol.

OUT Fast-track extradition would no longer be possible to or from the EU countries without the EAW and cases could be held up for years. Britain could apply to join Europol just like non-EU members Norway and Switzerland which cooperate fully and have liaison officers at the headquarters.

KEY STATS From 2009 to 2013, 507 suspects were sent to the UK using the EAW including sixty-three for child sex offences, 105 for drug trafficking and forty-four for murder; 4,005 suspects were extradited from the UK using EAWs to other EU states, including fifty-seven for child sex offences, 414 for drug trafficking and 105 for murder.

Rachid Ramda, an Algerian granted asylum in Britain, was the UK's longest-serving extradition prisoner by the time he was finally deported in 2005 to face terrorism charges laid ten years earlier in France, following a series of bomb attacks on the Paris Metro that left eight dead and 170 injured. The case caused diplomatic tensions between Britain and France as Ramda's lawyers, funded by Legal Aid, launched a series of appeals to delay his deportation. He was eventually jailed in France for ten years for association with a terrorist organisation. Cases like this helped to convince EU justice and home affairs ministers to agree a fast-track extradition measure, the European Arrest Warrant (EAW), following the 9/11 attacks in the US. It was hailed as a breakthrough in the fight against terror. 'There will be nowhere in Europe for terrorists to hide,' wrote Peter Hain, the Europe Minister, in October 2001. In stark contrast to the Ramda case, Hussain Osman, one of the would-be London bombers in the failed attacks of 21 July 2005, was seized on a European Arrest Warrant by Italian police in Rome and extradited back to Britain less than two months after he fled the country. It was not just terrorists, however, who were targeted by the warrant. By far the highest number of EAWs are issued by former Communist countries with very different justice systems to Britain: Poland tops the list with 3,090 warrants (until 2012/13) followed by Lithuania (438), and the Czech Republic (265). Suspects have been demanded under these fast-track measures for the theft of two car tyres, possession of 0.45g of cannabis and piglet-rustling (in Lithuania). Under the terms of the warrant, the country receiving the demand cannot normally refuse to make an arrest and hand over the suspect. Besides the trivial cases, the group Fair Trials International has campaigned to raise awareness of a growing number of miscarriages of justice involving Britons. Edmond Arapi was targeted by an Italian EAW to serve sixteen years in prison after being convicted *in absentia* of a murder in Genoa, a city he had never visited and which took place on a day he was at work in a café in Leek in Staffordshire. Italy only dropped the EAW after he had spent weeks in custody and several months on strict bail conditions. Andrew Symeou was extradited to Greece in July 2009 in connection with the death of a man at a nightclub, despite evidence that the charges were based on statements extracted by Greek police through intimidation of witnesses who later retracted their statements. Symeou was bailed after spending more than ten months in a Greek prison and was not finally cleared until June 2011. Deborah Dark was acquitted of drug offences in France in 1989 but, unknown to her, French prosecutors appealed and a two-year jail sentence was imposed in her absence. She was arrested in 2006 and only after a three-year legal ordeal was the case dropped. Patrick Connor (a pseudonym) was arrested in Spain with two friends in connection with two counterfeit €50 notes found in the apartment where they were staying. Released and returned to the UK, he was arrested under an EAW four years later and extradited back to Spain. He was held in a maximum security prison in Madrid and faced the prospect of a two-year wait in pre-trial detention. Although he maintained he had no knowledge of the counterfeit notes, he decided to plead guilty to reduce his time being held and spent nine weeks in prison before coming home to finish his studies with his life blighted by a criminal record. The potential dangers of the EAW, as well as its fundamental clash with the principles of British justice, were highlighted by a former member of the Commons Home Affairs Select

Committee during the passage of the 2003 Extradition Bill which enshrined the warrant into British law. The young MP spoke out against the way that it abolished the principle of 'dual criminality' by obliging EU states to extradite suspects for misdemeanours that are not considered criminal offences in the arresting country's own law. 'We are in new territory here. Never before have we given up the dual criminality protection,' David Cameron told the Commons while still a backbencher. 'I believe that we are making a great mistake … It is an important safeguard that people in this country have had for years.'

EU involvement in criminal justice measures has long been a bone of contention between Britain and Brussels despite a general acceptance that the police in Europe need to work closely together to combat complicated cases of cross-border crime. A clear policy of inter-governmental cooperation was set down in the Maastricht Treaty to ensure that member states retained a veto over measures that encroached on their own traditions of criminal justice. However, just fifteen years later the Lisbon Treaty dramatically increased EU control over policing and criminal law, moving the entire policy area into the realm of Qualified Majority Voting and oversight by the European Court of Justice. Because this was such a significant shift from a situation so carefully negotiated by British diplomats at Maastricht to avoid making British justice subject to a higher EU legal authority, the UK was given a one-off opportunity to decide whether to retain or reject all of the policing and criminal justice measures passed before the Lisbon Treaty entered into force. The government had until June 2014 to decide whether to opt out of 133 separate items, including the European Arrest Warrant, and afterwards negotiate to re-enter individual provisions on a case-by-case basis, at the risk of extra conditions being imposed by the EU. It was a golden opportunity in the eyes of Conservative backbenchers to repatriate powers from Brussels.

Theresa May, the Home Secretary, decided to exercise the block opt-out and opt back into thirty-five policies deemed to be in the national interest, despite their move to tighter EU control. These include the EAW as well as membership of Eurojust and Europol, two organisations based in The Hague. Eurojust, set up in 2002, exists to foster cooperation between national prosecuting authorities in crimes that concern more than one EU state. Member nations are obliged to provide Eurojust with 'any information necessary for the performance of its tasks'. The Lisbon Treaty has introduced the possibility of enabling Eurojust to initiate criminal investigations. Europol, the European Police Office headed by Rob Wainwright, a Welshman, became operational in 1999 and collects, stores, analyses and exchanges information, while also having the power to ask member states to initiate, conduct or coordinate criminal investigations. Europol and Eurojust coordination has been central to breaking international drugs and people-trafficking gangs as well as two global paedophile rings in joint police investigations known as Operation Koala and Operation Rescue. Koala began when a child abuse video was discovered in Australia that had been made in Belgium by an Italian producer with 2,500 global customers. It led to coordinated arrests including men in trusted positions, such as teachers and swimming instructors, as well as the identification of twenty-three children aged under sixteen. Operation Rescue led to the arrest of 184 suspected paedophiles, including 121 in the UK, when Dutch police seized the servers of a chatroom after British police traced two perpetrators to Spain and discovered their use of the website. The three-year operation across thirty countries led to the rescue of 230 children, including sixty in the UK. These are the kind of transnational inquiries which show the benefits of EU coordination.

The Fresh Start group of Conservative MPs called for Britain to take the opportunity of the Lisbon Treaty opt-out to withdraw completely from the field of criminal justice involvement with the EU. 'The UK has a unique legal tradition and should not be subject to ECJ rulings in the area of Policing and Criminal Justice (PCJ),' the group said in its manifesto in November 2013. 'The Lisbon Treaty provided the UK with an option to opt out of 133 EU laws, which the government plans to invoke. We should go further and opt out of all EU PCJ laws entirely, and pursue operational cooperation with the EU via other means.' Bilateral cooperation would be possible with Europol, which works closely with non-EU members Norway and Switzerland, and has officials from these two countries permanently based at Europol headquarters. But other measures, such as the European Arrest Warrant, would be difficult to recreate on a voluntary basis. The Fresh Start proposal was dismissed by the Liberal Democrat spokeswoman on justice, Sarah Ludford.

> These proposals would indeed be a fresh start, for the thousands of criminals who would find it far easier to escape justice. Pulling out of EU crime-fighting measures altogether would be a gift to drug-smugglers, human-traffickers and online sex offenders. The European Arrest Warrant does need reform, but we should not throw the baby out with the bath water. It remains a vital crime-fighting tool that has prevented thousands of criminals from escaping the long arm of the law.

The Association of Chief Police Officers (ACPO) called the EAW the most important of all the EU measures. In parliamentary evidence, it wrote:

> Recent data gathered by the Metropolitan Police Service (MPS) in the first quarter of 2012 showed that of 61,939 people arrested in London, 8,089 were nationals from EU countries (13 per cent) and 9,358 were foreign nationals from outside the EU (15 per cent). In 2011–12 the MPS received fifty EAWs for homicide, twenty for rape, and ninety for robbery. Each of these cases represents a person who is wanted for a serious crime who fled to the UK. There is strong evidence to show that foreign criminals who come to the UK continue to offend when in the UK. There is a real risk that opting out of the EAW and relying on less effective extradition

arrangements could have the effect of turning the UK
into a 'safe haven' for Europe's criminals.

By including the European Arrest Warrant in the measures Britain decided to retain, Theresa May also agreed
to accept another controversial EU justice measure,
the European Supervision Order (ESO), as a safeguard
against mistreatment. The ESO is an alternative to pre-
trial detention and allows the home state of the suspect
to request supervision measures rather than see its citizens locked up for months, like Andrew Symeou. The
British government had long been in two minds about
agreeing it because the UK receives far more EAW
requests than it makes. It was a demonstration of how a
further EU measure was thought necessary to ameliorate
an earlier one. In retaining the EAW, May introduced
several safeguards, including another EU measure, the
European Investigation Order – an alternative to the
arrest warrant which obliges police and prosecutors to
share evidence before any extradition. She also legislated
so that British judges can refuse an EAW for minor
crimes, referring to the Connor banknote case, and
amended the Extradition Act to ensure suspects can only
be extradited once a decision to charge has been made,
referring to the Symeou case.

But the British government refused point blank to
sign up to another criminal justice measure provided
for in the Lisbon Treaty and proposed by the European
Commission in 2013 – a European Public Prosecutor.

This office, run through Eurojust, would 'be responsible for investigating, prosecuting and bringing to judgment … the perpetrators of, and accomplices in, offences against the Union's financial interests', according to the treaty. Although Britain has made clear it will opt out, the European Public Prosecutor can go ahead under 'enhanced agreement' by at least nine member states. The Lisbon Treaty also made provision for the EPP's role to be expanded in the future 'to include serious cross-border crime', suggesting the foundations of a common EU system of criminal justice. 'There is nothing wrong with practical cooperation with other European countries on policing and criminal justice matters, especially when crime is increasingly international,' said Theresa May. 'But there is no reason at all for a European Public Prosecutor or anything like a European police force. We will make sure that Britain does not participate and will not come under the jurisdiction of any such prosecutor.' Britain has consistently been a reluctant partner in EU justice and policing measures. It will try to avoid the most intrusive developments if it stays in the EU, and will try to cooperate on the most vital measures if it leaves.

OVERSEAS AID

IN The UK counts the proportion of its EU membership fee spent on overseas development towards its national aid target of 0.7 per cent of gross national income (GNI). In 2014, £1.14 billion of the £11.73 billion spent on aid by the UK was managed through the European Commission, comprising £816 million through the EU budget and £328 million through the European Development Fund.[53]

OUT Britain could keep its target of spending 0.7 per cent of GNI on overseas development and could still coordinate spending with the European Commission, or it could divert the £1.14 billion that goes to aid through Brussels back to domestic spending.

KEY STATS Britain is the world's second most generous international donor country by amount and fifth most generous by percentage of GNI. The EU and its member states together provided €55.2 billion in international aid in 2012, more than half of the global total and 0.43 per cent of collective gross national income. The EU itself handed out €9.54 billion from its budget. The top recipient was Turkey with €419 million, then the Palestinian Territories with €247 million, Afghanistan €200 million, Ethiopia €193 million and Serbia €186 million.[54]

The South African government reacted angrily when Britain announced in 2013 that it would end direct aid to the country in 2015. Although the annual grant was only £19 million, a tiny fraction of the UK's £11.73 billion annual overseas development spending, Pretoria's Department of International Relations said that it was 'tantamount to redefining our relationship'.

Partly this was because it brought an abrupt end to an era of British assistance for a close fellow Commonwealth member, and partly it was because South Africa felt itself a victim of domestic political wrangling over the aid budget after surviving a cull of British partners in 2011, which ended assistance to Angola, Bosnia and Herzegovina, Burundi, Cameroon, Cambodia, China, Gambia, Indonesia, Iraq, Kosovo, Lesotho, Moldova, Niger, Russia, Serbia and Vietnam. They were followed by India in another sudden announcement in 2012 that the £280 million annual transfer from the UK would end in 2015. These countries were now deemed to fall into the 'middle income' category or even 'upper middle income' and in times of hardship the UK government decided to focus its overseas aid strategically on reducing poverty in twenty-six of the world's poorest and most fragile countries. The writing had been on the wall for months for India after its finance minister Pranab Mukherjee, later the country's President, said that Britain's aid payment was 'a peanut in our total development expenditure'. In contrast to South Africa, the Indian External Affairs Minister Salman Khurshid accepted the British decision by declaring that 'aid is past, trade is future'. Britain's aid budget will be kept at the ring-fenced level of 0.7 per cent of gross national income, one of only five EU countries (all rich northerners) to reach the level set as a target for 2015. 'South Africa has made enormous progress over the past two decades, to the extent that it is now the region's economic powerhouse and Britain's biggest trading partner in Africa. South Africa is now in a position to fund its own development,' said Justine Greening, the International Development Secretary. 'It is right that our relationship changes to one of mutual co-operation and trade.' Aid agencies disagreed. Melanie Ward of ActionAid said:

> The UK, and particularly David Cameron, rightly state a desire to end extreme poverty. This is incredibly important, but running away from middle-income countries where 80 per cent live on less than $2 a day is the wrong way to make this happen. This is the wrong decision, at the wrong time. It is particularly concerning since it comes hot on the heels of the UK announcing its early withdrawal of aid from India.

Some British funding will still find its way to most of the countries on the list of those being dropped by the Department for International Development (DFID), however. That is because they will get cash from the European Union. The proportion of Britain's EU membership fee related to EU aid spending is counted towards the national development spending target, as is the money sent from DFID to the European Development Fund (EDF), an intergovernmental agreement by the EU states outside the EU budget, beyond the control of the European Parliament and the main vehicle for EU funding of African, Caribbean and Pacific countries. In 2014, £1.14 billion spent on aid by the UK was managed through the European Commission, made up of £816 million through the EU budget and

£328 million through the EDF. But even in Brussels, the winds of change are blowing through its huge overseas aid budget in a major shake-up that could also see both South Africa and India losing out on annual direct funding.

Britain's commitment to spending 0.7 per cent of national wealth on international aid has been controversial among politicians, mainly on the Right, who believe that the money would be better off spent on schools and healthcare in the UK. Lord Ashcroft, the Tory peer, said that many Conservatives found the level of aid spending 'morally wrong' when the government was cutting domestic budgets. He sent an open letter to Ms Greening on her appointment to urge her to 'turn off the golden taps and stop flooding the developing world with our money'. Conservatives argued that India's decision to choose French Mirage jets over UK-made Typhoons showed that aid spending was not bringing Britain associated political benefits. Godfrey Bloom, the former UK Independence Party MEP, had his own criticism of overseas aid. 'How we can possibly be giving a billion pounds a month, when we're in this sort of debt, to Bongo Bongo Land is completely beyond me,' he was filmed telling party activists. 'To buy Ray-Ban sunglasses, apartments in Paris, Ferraris and all the rest of it that goes with most of the foreign aid. F18s for Pakistan. We need a new squadron of F18s. Who's got the squadrons? Pakistan, where we send the money.' Bloom was asked by his party to stop using the phrase Bongo Bongo Land but insisted that he was not being racist. 'If anybody would care to take a look at the Oxford dictionary ... they would find bongo is a white antelope that lives in the forest,' he said. Bloom told *The Times* he had received three letters of support from Africa for his remarks and asked, 'Is my mailbag lying to me?'

Yet even Kofi Annan, the former United Nations Secretary General, supported calls for Britain and the EU to stop giving billions of pounds in aid to wealthier countries.

> The emerging markets and the countries that are doing well should wean themselves off aid. Countries like Brazil, China, India, Ghana, Guatemala and Honduras – some of these countries can fend for themselves. In fact, I have had the chance to suggest to some of them that they should not accept Britain's aid willingly. They need to say 'We are full enough', so that there will be more money available for the really poor and weaker.

The EU's treaties give it the power to conduct a common policy in overseas aid and humanitarian assistance without preventing its member states from conducting their own actions in these areas. The top priority of the EU is to 'foster the sustainable economic, social and environmental development of developing countries, with the primary aim of eradicating poverty'. This is a good fit with Britain's overarching aims in the areas of development cooperation and humanitarian aid which are, respectively, to eliminate poverty and to respond effectively to disasters. The treaties also require the EU to

contribute to peace, security, the sustainable development of the earth, solidarity and mutual respect among
peoples, free and fair trade, eradication of poverty and
the protection of human rights, in particular the rights
of the child as well as to the strict observance and the
development of international law, including respect for
the principles of the United Nations Charter.

The European Consensus on Development agreed in
2006 stated that the overarching aim of EU development
policy was to reduce poverty worldwide by achieving the
Millennium Development Goals (MDGs), a set of eight
targets agreed at the United Nations in 2000 for 2015.
However, some of the world's poorest countries were
a long way off the key MDGs, causing Britain's review
of aid partners to focus funds and triggering a rethink
in Brussels. The first sign of this was the European
Commission's Agenda for Change review of 2011 which
also began to suggest that 'Middle Income Countries'
like India and South Africa should lose direct aid as their
economies continued to grow. It signalled a shift to assistance based on good governance, democracy and human
rights, linked to greater conditionality; and also based on
growth, with a strong focus on leveraging private sector
money. Neighbouring countries, especially those ambitious to join the EU, will continue to receive generous
support from Brussels, which is why Britain could end its
direct payments to Bosnia, Moldova, Serbia and Kosovo
in the knowledge that the UK will actually still be funding
development through its contribution to the EU budget.

It is easy for the media to find bizarre projects and misspent funds in the EU's vast overseas funding operation, with €58.7 billion earmarked for the 2014–20 budget period, a rise of 3.3 per cent on the previous seven years. In 2012, the *Sunday Telegraph* highlighted the fact that the EU spent around half of its aid budget on middle-income countries, with £30 million spent that year in China on twenty-two projects, £10 million in Brazil, £9.5 million in Argentina and £40 million in Russia, including £240,000 for an arts project in St Petersburg. Iceland received £4.2 million including £400,000 for a scheme to promote tourism in Katla national park while projects in Turkey, the biggest recipient of EU aid, included funding for a TV series about the EU. The paper did not mention the EU's Food Facility programme which paid for the inoculation of 44.6 million livestock in the poorest countries, the €25 million spent towards a solar power plant in Burkina Faso to provide power to 400,000 people, or the programme to provide basic primary education to 40,000 Somali children and train 4,000 primary and secondary school teachers in Somalia.[55] The European Commission's overseas aid directorate said:

> Investing in external assistance is a smart investment, with a long-term vision. The EU and its partners have a mutual interest in making sure poverty steps back: less poverty means less trafficking, less illegal migration, less pandemics, less terrorism and insecurity. It is cheaper to eliminate root causes of the problem than to deal

with the symptoms further down the line. In the current context, it makes more sense than ever to improve coordination of all member states' aid: we will avoid duplication and get the highest impact.

But while DFID rated aid delivered through the European Development Fund as 'very good value for money' because of its 'strong poverty focus with 85 per cent of funds going to lower income countries', delivery through the EU budget was only rated 'adequate value for money for UK aid' because 'a significant share of resources goes to middle income countries and focus on MDGs is mixed; procedures are inflexible'.

Development cooperation was the subject of one of the first batch of the government's assessment of Britain's relationship with the EU known as the Review of the Balance of Consequences and published in July 2013. The consensus of most respondents was that 'while there is a need for improvement in many areas of EU activity, the advantages of working through the EU outweigh the disadvantages', according to the government's summary. The Trades Union Congress (TUC), for example, said that criticism levelled at the EU 'makes the case for improvement, not repatriation' of powers to the national level. If these powers were returned, 'the UK would achieve less with its expenditure than it did now, and the activities of EU member states put together would also achieve less'. Only two out of fifty-one submissions questioned the value of working through the EU in development cooperation. Open

Europe recommended that national contributions to the EU aid budget should be made entirely voluntary on a similar basis to the European Development Fund (EDF). The Freedom Association argued that EU aid spending has been wasteful, ineffective and harmful to the UK's objectives. It argued that the UK could achieve its development goals more effectively if it were to take more action bilaterally, or even through other multilateral channels independent of the EU. Outside the EU, the Swiss Agency for Development and Cooperation (SDC), told the review that it had an input into EU aid policy debates through contacts with the European Commission as well as a close working relationship with four key donor countries in the EU including the UK. Switzerland established its development priorities in consultation with the European Commission to make sure its aid effort was aligned with the EU. This would almost certainly be the case with Britain if it were to leave the EU, especially given that both Labour in government and the Conservatives have been keen to commit to generous aid spending both through Brussels and bilaterally.

TRANSPORT

IN British airlines are able to fly not only to and from other EU states but also between airports within those states. Budget airlines owe their existence to EU deregulation.

OUT British airlines would have to renegotiate both intra-EU flight rights and transatlantic slots. Its road hauliers would still have to comply with EU rules on safety, size, loading and drivers' hours when working on the continent.

KEY STATS Heathrow is the EU's busiest airport with 73.4 million passengers in 2014, followed by Paris Charles De Gaulle (63.6 million) and Frankfurt (59.4 million).[56] Dover is the EU's busiest passenger port and Felixstowe the seventh busiest container port. More than 21 million passengers travelled through the Channel Tunnel in 2014.[57] Almost 70 million passengers flew with easyJet in 2014–15 on 735 routes in thirty-one countries, with ninety more routes planned in 2016.[58]

The Irish government refused to allow Tony Ryan's new airline permission to fly from Dublin to Luton in order to protect the national carrier, Aer Lingus, from competition on the lucrative route between Ireland and Britain. Margaret Thatcher's government had other ideas. The British Prime Minister had pushed for the Single Market which ushered in the 'double disapproval' regime, meaning that authorities in both countries had to object to stop an airline opening up flights between them. It was a weakening of national sovereignty that

Thatcher very much approved of. Ryanair was given the green light to fly to Luton by the British authorities and ended up eventually becoming bigger than Aer Lingus and embroiled in a long-running battle to take it over. Ironically, the EU authorities blocked this on the grounds of maintaining healthy competition in the interests of consumers. Successive rounds of EU deregulation broke down national airline monopolies and made it possible for Ryanair and its British rival easyJet to get off the ground. They are now Europe's two biggest low-cost carriers. 'EasyJet is a child of the EU,' said the company's spokesman. 'Essentially aviation was controlled by each sovereign state and easyJet broke down historic sovereignty-based agreements.' Michael O'Leary, the outspoken chief executive of Ryanair, put it like this: 'We've liberated people to fly. We've done more for European integration than any other company. We've probably prevented wars breaking out because we make it easier for young kids to spend time travelling abroad.' The benefits for consumers have been substantial. Before Ryanair came along in 1986, it cost £170 to fly from Dublin to London return with either Aer Lingus or British Airways, the only two options. Ryanair immediately halved the price, forcing its rivals to cut fares too. The era of budget air travel had dawned and has been one of the great success stories of the EU's Single Market. The European Common Aviation Area means that an airline based in any member state can fly between any two airports in the EU, including between airports within a single EU country. Most countries jealously guard their airspace rights, which is why European airlines cannot fly between US cities and US airlines cannot fly from one European airport to another European airport. Despite Michael O'Leary once calling the European Commission the 'evil empire' when it challenged subsidies apparently provided by Charleroi airport in Belgium, in November 2015 he said: 'We are very actively supporting the campaign to keep the UK in the European Union ... We need the UK to stay a committed member of Europe just to keep some kind of more sensible economic approach.'

Cheap airline travel is one clear benefit of the EU that is probably here to stay thanks to the level of intense competition unleashed by the Single Market and pioneered most aggressively by Ryanair. The biggest immediate impact of Brexit is likely to be on British airlines and their ability to hold on to lucrative overseas routes, including across the Atlantic, and this in turn could affect fares depending on the final outcome of lengthy and difficult renegotiations. In order to keep the status quo, the UK would either have to follow non-member Norway into the European Economic Area (EEA) which will maintain access to the European Common Aviation Area (ECAA) or negotiate from outside the EEA to stay in the ECAA, membership of which has to be ratified by every EU member state. In either case, Britain would then have to agree to the full application of EU aviation law and abide by decisions taken by the EU affecting how the ECAA is run without having a vote on them. ECAA membership gives British airlines cabotage rights – the ability to fly between EU airports without having to start or end at a British airport. Without membership of the ECAA, easyJet would still be able to fly from the UK to a European destination and back again but the loss of intra-EU routes would probably force it to create a new subsidiary based inside the EU if it wanted to carry on with those flights. Such a split into two companies could have an impact on fares and on employment levels at easyJet's Luton base. Ryanair, which is headquartered in Ireland, would still be able to fly to and from the UK.

Leaving the EU would also require British airlines to renegotiate transatlantic routes which have been agreed in an EU-wide package between Brussels and the US. Brexit would signal a period of turbulence for airlines and government aviation officials with the EU and beyond. 'If the UK was willing to accept every aspect of the [EU] single aviation market, it would presumably be possible to negotiate reciprocal access,' wrote Handley Stevens, former Under Secretary at the Ministry of Transport in an essay for Regent's University.

> However, air service negotiations are famous for hard bargaining, and European airlines which had lost market share to UK airlines (notably to easyJet) might well look for ways to restore their competitive edge, for example by insisting that UK airlines could only fly to and from the UK. The renegotiation of bilateral rights with third countries such as the USA could be even more difficult. The rights of UK airlines under EU agreements would

expire if not with immediate effect from the date of with-drawal, when BA and Virgin Atlantic would cease to be EU airlines, then at best after the usual period of twelve months' notice. Moreover, in any renegotiations aris-ing from such a disengagement, against a tight deadline which might apply to a large number of simultaneous negotiations, it cannot be assumed that the third coun-tries concerned would necessarily be prepared to grant unchanged rights to UK airlines under a new bilateral treaty without demanding significant additional benefits for their own airlines in exchange.

The ultimate impact on the consumer is unclear, and may be minimal, but the upheaval for the airlines could be considerable.

For travel by road, British companies that run commercial vehicles on the continent would still have to comply with EU rules for driver working hours and rest periods, as well as the common regulations for pollution and vehicle weight and size, notwithstand-ing any changes to these rules for Britain's roads after leaving the EU. The British government has already rejected so-called 'super lorries' measuring up to 25.25 metres long after the European Commission left it up to national authorities to decide whether to allow lorries beyond the existing 18.75 metres and 44 tonnes gross vehicle weight maximums. One advantage of leav-ing the EU claimed by Brexit campaigners would be to charge foreign lorries to drive on British roads. Charging road users is not illegal under EU law at the moment, provided that the charge is also paid by domestic drivers. Following pressure from the Bavarian Christian Social Union party in the ruling German coalition, the government is planning to charge all vehicles and compensate domestic road users by a lower road tax. It remains to be seen whether the European Commission will challenge this blatant attempt to circumvent the spirit of EU law. If an independent Britain brought in a surcharge on European lorries while exempting its own, the European Commission has made it clear that there would probably be repercussions. 'If the UK, in the event that it was outside the EU, decided to introduce legislation which discriminates against foreigners, it would expose itself to the risk of countervailing measures from the EU member states, which could end up being very costly for British hauliers,' said an official at the European Commission transport directorate.

Transport policy is one area where a supra-national body like the EU has a genuine role in facilitating common standards for a continent criss-crossed by rail services, roads, waterways and aviation routes. While the impact of Brexit would be felt most keenly in the aviation sector, which has the highest international dimension of British transport, it would have much less effect on other modes of transport where the vast majority of journeys begin and end in the UK. For travel by train, the UK only has two international routes (through the Channel Tunnel and from Belfast to Dublin) covered primarily by several international agreements including the Intergovernmental Organisation for International

Carriage by Rail (OTIF), originally founded in 1893 and of which Britain is one of forty-eight members. This sets basic rules for technical standards, compensation for delayed passengers and carriage of dangerous goods. For travel by sea, general standards for safety, training, pollution and working conditions are set globally by the International Maritime Organisation (which the UK has been a member of since 1949) and the International Labour Organisation (of which the UK was a founder member in 1919). In contrast to the potentially massive upheaval for UK-based airlines, British sea and rail travel would not change much in the event of Brexit.

CONCLUSION

When a referendum was called on its constitutional future, opinion polls in Australia were clear for months that the country would ditch the monarchy and become a republic. Yet on the day, every state voted to keep the Queen. The existing system was not widely liked, but campaigners for the monarchy helped to swing the result their way by focusing on what would replace it (an appointed head of state, when none of the potential candidates enjoyed much support). It was a classic lesson in how to overcome instinctive calls for change and maintain the status quo in a referendum – by moving the argument beyond the failings of the current system to debating what the alternatives could really mean. It was a tactic used so remorselessly by the Better Together campaign in the Scottish independence referendum that it earned the nickname Project Fear. Just as there were broad objections to the monarchy in the run-up to the referendum Down Under, there are similarly pervasive feelings of antipathy towards the European Union in the UK. The EU is regarded by many as bureaucratic, remote, lacking democratic account-ability and wasteful – for the twenty-first year in a row, auditors gave an 'adverse opinion' on its accounts due to multiple 'errors' resulting in €6.5 billion being misspent in 2014 alone. In the EU's own Eurobarometer opinion poll published in December 2015, just 23 per cent of the British said they trusted the EU, with only Cyprus and Greece polling lower, and only 17 per cent of British respondents said they thought the EU was going in the right direction (five countries were even lower, including Greece and France). Successive crises have brought the EU to its knees and demonstrated that it can barely cope with the big challenges of the modern world: the euro crisis saw Greece plunged into a six-year recession, while high levels of youth unemployment persist in half a dozen eurozone countries pressurised to adopt tough austerity measures; the migrant crisis exposed a spectacular inability to coordinate an effective response, jeopardising both security and the future of the borderless continental travel area.

The EU has plenty of faults. But will a reflection on the practical implications of leaving be decisive in determining whether, as in Australia, voters stick with the devil they know?

This book has assessed the areas where the EU impacts most upon the UK. It has highlighted instances where the EU has been beneficial to communities in Britain, for example ensuring generous subsidies to reward farming and support regional development through good economic times and bad. It has also highlighted huge bureaucratic costs for business and industry such as the Working Time and Reach (chemicals) directives that would not have been devised by MPs in Westminster but were unavoidable due to EU membership. No system of governance is perfect and no one will agree with every law passed, which is why, at the national level, political parties are regularly voted in and out as the pendulum of public opinion swings for or against a particular choice of administration. One of the fundamental complaints about the EU, however, is that its form of democracy does not work like that. There is no pendulum. Whichever political movement is in the ascendant in the European Parliament, whoever is appointed to the role of European Commissioner and whichever national governments are represented in the European Council, the EU bandwagon seems to roll on in broadly the same direction of greater integration. As Günter Verheugen, the German member of the European Commission from 1999 to 2009, observed (before Croatia brought the membership total to twenty-eight nations):

> There are twenty-seven commissioners, which means twenty-seven directorate-generals. And twenty-seven directorate-generals means that everyone needs to prove that they are needed by constantly producing new directives, strategies or projects. In any case, the rule is: More and more, more and more, all the time.

To be fair, Jean-Claude Juncker, who became President of the European Commission in 2014, made a determined start on cutting the notorious levels of red tape produced in Brussels by putting a vice-president in charge of a better regulation agenda, proposing just twenty-three new initiatives for 2016 following an average of 130 a year under his predecessor José Manuel Barroso, and attempting to focus clearly on promoting jobs, growth and investment. In another change of approach, Juncker also proposed withdrawing a number of initiatives as well as announcing a review of key areas of legislation such as workplace health and safety 'to ensure they are fit for purpose'. This all fitted in handily with one of the four goals of David Cameron's renegotiation – to cut bureaucracy and kill the urge to produce 'more and more, all the time'. The Prime Minister's other three renegotiation points were also aimed at giving some measure of comfort to wavering voters looking for better protection from Margaret Thatcher's warning about the dangers of a 'European super-state exercising a new dominance from Brussels'. The safeguards for non-eurozone nations from group voting by the euro countries are a sensible move to reassure those who fear that the entire EU project could become driven by the needs of saving the single currency, as well as giving a group of more eurosceptic countries a form of emergency brake on legislation. Similarly, a 'red card' for national parliaments is a step towards returning power to national capitals, even if experience of the 'yellow card' suggests that the measure will hardly ever be used, while it remains to be seen if the end of the commitment to 'ever closer union' applying to Britain will have more than a powerful symbolic importance; and again only time will tell if toughening up restrictions on certain welfare benefits for EU citizens will have a significant effect on net migration to Britain.

How to vote, then, when the referendum comes? This book has shown that in many of the key themes and sectors affected by EU membership, there are strong arguments on both sides of the fence. The weight of argument on Britain's place in the world is that it would be diminished by leaving, an inevitable effect of detachment from a regional power, and perhaps the unavoidable fate anyway of a cash-strapped medium-sized country in the process of downsizing its armed forces and global diplomatic presence. If Britain was to leave the EU, inward investment may well fall, putting thousands of jobs at risk and threatening national income. But the negative impact in these areas will be negligible if Britain remains in the Single Market like Norway, or agrees a comprehensive Free Trade Agreement upon departure to retain open trading links. Unfortunately for voters, the precise nature of Britain's post-EU relationship will not be clear at the point of voting, adding another layer of uncertainty to an already complicated choice. If there were to be no penalties for leaving, other net contributor countries such as Sweden and Denmark could also be tempted to flee, meaning that Brussels will make sure that there are consequences for the first nation to call it a day.

The EU nation which will feel the largest impact, however, will be Britain's nearest neighbour, Ireland. A report by the respected Economic and Social Research Unit, based in Dublin, said in November 2015 that a

Brexit 'could reduce bilateral trade flows between Ireland and the UK by 20 per cent or more' if Britain failed to remain part of the EU's Single Market and trade barriers were reimposed. It added that: 'While the 20 per cent estimate is an average figure, the impact would differ significantly across sectors, products and firm types as merchandise trade in particular is heavily concentrated in some sectors and products ... and any barriers to trade would increase prices of UK imports to Ireland.' The economy of Northern Ireland would also be vulnerable to a return to trading barriers, the report warned.

As mentioned in the Sovereignty chapter, the impact of Brexit could be also be dramatically felt on the other side of the Irish Sea if it triggers a second independence referendum in Scotland. Although the EU vote is on Britain's relationship with its European neighbours, concern about the internal relations of the UK could well become a major factor for many voters.

Some of the benefits to be gained from leaving the EU that seemed obvious just a few years ago are a little less clear-cut today. The Common Fisheries Policy has long been a by-word for atrocious EU governance but has finally undergone reforms that seem to promise better management, closer to regional needs and more responsive to scientific advice. On international trade, the European Commission failed for years to press forward with far-reaching Free Trade Agreements but seems at long last to have woken up to the world beyond its border region. The TTIP deal being negotiated with the US could finally demonstrate that there are substantial benefits from trusting the EU with the responsibility for international trade policy. It will not convince many eurosceptics, who point out that the EU has failed to achieve a free trade deal with any of the top five non-European economies in the world (US, China, Japan, Brazil and India). Closer to home, the EU rushed into green targets and mechanisms to combat climate change that have so far proved costly failures, such as the Emissions Trading System. There are some signs that a more realistic balance is being struck, including the decision to leave fracking to national governments and to back off from charging all airlines for emissions for the whole of any flight into the EU. Only time will tell if Brussels can find the right blend of climate- and business-friendly green policies.

Some advocates of an EU membership based mainly around trade argue that like-minded voters who want more far-reaching reforms to Britain's relationship than those presented by David Cameron should vote to leave, so that the EU is shocked into further concessions to prevent Britain's departure. The 'real renegotiation' could then begin followed by a second referendum on a radically changed form of membership. Cameron has sought to quash this idea, not least because it might tempt undecided voters to join the 'leave' camp. In his Chatham House speech, the Prime Minister insisted:

> This is a huge decision for our country, perhaps the biggest we will make in our lifetimes. And it will be the final decision. So to those who suggest that a decision in

the referendum to leave would merely produce another stronger renegotiation and then a second referendum in which Britain would stay, I say think again. The renegotiation is happening right now. And the referendum that follows will be a once-in-a-generation choice ... If we vote to leave, then we will leave. There will not be another renegotiation and another referendum.

This reflects the legal position that a vote for Brexit would lead Britain to trigger Article 50 of the Lisbon Treaty, the exit clause for a country wishing to leave the EU. It allows two years to negotiate a new relationship, which could be extended if both sides agree. However, history shows that a referendum that goes against the grain of the EU is usually followed by a second attempt, including Denmark's re-run rejection of the Maastricht Treaty (it voted for it second time after receiving four opt-outs), Norway's two attempts at joining (rejected both times), and Ireland's rejections of the Nice and Lisbon Treaties (both passed second time after extra guarantees). When the proposed EU Constitution was rejected by France and the Netherlands in 2005, almost all the changes were repackaged into the Lisbon Treaty of 2009. Legally, Cameron is right to warn against a second referendum with a better offer to Britain following an initial 'leave' vote but past form suggests it is possible – albeit a very high-risk option for those voters who fundamentally want to stay in the EU.

What, then, would be the positive advantages of leaving? Primarily it would mean opting out of the European political project, so that all legislative decisions and judicial oversight will once again be based on the British Isles – provided that membership of the Single Market through the European Economic Area is also rejected. If the UK left the EU only to join the EEA, then legislative decisions over farming, fishing, justice, policing, international trade policy, regional funding, transport, VAT and customs will return to these shores and become subject to UK courts, while employment and social regulations, the four freedoms, state aid, competition and consumer affairs policy, and most environmental regulation would stay under the EU and the European Court of Justice. As they mark their referendum ballot paper to stay or leave, voters are unlikely to know what the UK's post-EU status will be. It means in practice that only those comfortable with being outside the EU and the EEA should vote for Brexit, in line with UKIP policy for a Free Trade Agreement with Brussels and nothing more.

A complete break of this kind means that Britain will be at liberty to reverse any EU rule or regulation accepted into domestic law. Many will not be removed because they protect air, food or water quality, or guarantee equal treatment for men and women in the workplace. An independent UK government will be free to introduce more 'flexibilities' for employers, such as scrapping the EU's minimum four-week paid annual holiday entitlement or abandoning the equal rights for agency workers after twelve weeks in a job. Other expensive requirements, such as holding open a post for a pregnant worker who leaves to have a baby, could be revoked for small and medium-sized businesses altogether. With the rest of the country freed from EU standards, the onus will be on exporters to ensure that they keep up to date with the latest technical and legal requirements agreed in Brussels if they want to trade with the continent. Whole areas of national life will return to domestic control, from regional funding to agricultural support to international trade policy – although any decision to cut tariffs to allow cheaper imports of food and other goods must be applied evenly to all markets under World Trade Organization rules. That will limit the ability to respond in kind to protectionist moves by Brussels following Brexit. VAT could be scrapped and replaced with a local sales tax to stimulate regional economies.

This book found that the sector most strongly against leaving the EU is the City of London. Under the 'complete break' scenario, thousands of jobs and billions of pounds in taxes could flee the country. The implications could be far-reaching – a drop in government income would need to be made up elsewhere, the withdrawal of significant support from wealthy bankers for the London property market could mean a house-price correction, and the long-term reduction in critical mass for the financial services industry could lead to a rebalancing of the British economy. For some, this provides ample reason for voting to leave the EU, while for others it will be a reason to stay.

In the end, the choice facing Britain boils down to a clash of fundamental forces. On the one hand there is the defence of national identity and sovereignty from a supranational political project where Britain's view by definition cannot always prevail, while on the other hand there is the belief that only joint govern-ance will ensure economic and national security in full partnership with Britain's neighbours. Many of those who passionately want to leave the EU subscribe to those analysts who foresee no financial damage to the national balance sheet, or indeed economic benefits from Brexit, while Nigel Farage has said that he would 'rather we weren't slightly richer' if Britain could regain full border controls. Many of those who passionately want the UK to play a full part in the EU see no other way to deal with globalisation than sharing sovereignty to build a mighty European bloc. Most British voters lie somewhere between these two positions, torn between the ideal of open European commerce and pulling up the drawbridge, with a feeling that in practice the EU experiment has gone too far.

Returning to sovereign control over domestic affairs and full responsibility for its destiny on the world stage, Britain's economy is robust enough to survive outside the EU despite the upheaval of leaving. The question is whether it will thrive – and whether departure will trig-ger the break-up not of the EU, but of the UK, with a new independence vote in Scotland.

This book has highlighted the wide range of shared concerns between the European nations and shown that some measure of compromise is inevitable in the face of so many competing national interests. Whatever the outcome of the referendum, every effort should be made to maintain the best possible working relations with the EU. No perfect formula exists for the complete jigsaw of continental cooperation and Britain has much to lose from an acrimonious breakdown in relations with the European Union, in or out.

BRITAIN'S EU CONTRIBUTIONS, REBATE AND RECEIPTS

Year	Gross total	Rebate	Gross contribution	Public sector receipts	Net contribution
1973	181	n/a	**181**	79	**102**
1974	181	n/a	**181**	150	**31**
1975	342	n/a	**342**	398	**56**
1976	463	n/a	**463**	296	**167**
1977	737	n/a	**737**	368	**369**
1978	1,348	n/a	**1,348**	526	**822**
1979	1,606	n/a	**1,606**	659	**947**
1980	1,767	98	**1,669**	963	**706**
1981	2,174	693	**1,481**	1,084	**397**
1982	2,863	1,019	**1,844**	1,238	**606**
1983	2,976	807	**2,169**	1,522	**647**
1984	3,204	528	**2,676**	2,020	**656**
1985	3,940	227	**3,713**	1,905	**1,808**
1986	4,493	1,701	**2,792**	2,220	**572**
1987	5,202	1,153	**4,049**	2,328	**1,721**
1988	5,138	1,594	**3,544**	2,182	**1,362**
1989	5,585	1,154	**4,431**	2,116	**2,315**
1990	6,355	1,697	**4,658**	2,183	**2,475**
1991	5,807	2,497	**3,309**	2,765	**544**
1992	6,738	1,881	**4,857**	2,827	**2,030**
1993	7,985	2,539	**5,446**	3,291	**2,155**
1994	7,189	1,726	**5,463**	3,253	**2,211**

1995	8,889	1,207	7,682	3,665	4,017
1996	9,133	2,412	6,721	4,373	2,348
1997	7,991	1,733	6,258	4,661	1,597
1998	10,090	1,378	8,712	4,115	4,597
1999	10,287	3,171	7,117	3,479	3,638
2000	10,517	2,085	8,433	4,241	4,192
2001	9,379	4,560	4,819	3,430	1,389
2002	9,439	3,099	6,340	3,201	3,139
2003	10,966	3,559	7,407	3,728	3,679
2004	10,895	3,593	7,302	4,294	3,008
2005	12,567	3,656	8,911	5,329	3,581
2006	12,426	3,569	8,857	4,948	3,909
2007	12,456	3,523	8,933	4,332	4,601
2008	12,653	4,862	7,791	4,497	3,294
2009	14,129	5,392	8,737	4,401	4,336
2010	15,197	3,047	12,150	4,768	7,382
2011	15,357	3,143	12,214	4,132	8,082
2012	15,746	3,110	12,636	4,169	8,467
2013	18,135	3,674	14,461	3,996	10,465
2014	18,777	4,416	14,361	4,576	9,785
2015	17,779	4,861	12,918	4,445	8,473
TOTAL	339,083	89,363	249,720	123,154	126,565

Notes: All figures in £ million. Figures for 2015 are estimated by the Treasury; rebate column includes ad hoc refunds from 1980 until 1984 and some of the 1985 total when the rebate officially started (total of pure rebate is £86,157 million). Net contribution figure £1 million out in some years due to rounding.

The total gross payment made by the UK before taking into account the rebate was put at £484.229 billion at the end of 2014 by Vote Leave, a campaign group for Brexit, by converting all contributions to June 2014 prices and using ONS figures. The total net payment over the 42-year period was put at £157.343 billion.

Sources: 'The EU Budget', House of Commons Library Standard Note SN/EP/864; 'European Union Finances 2015', HM Treasury CM 9167.

NOTES

All figures correct at time of printing but subject to change as budgets are revised or updated. Historic budget figures given in prices of the day. Quotations taken from a range of authoritative sources including media reports, speeches and books listed in the bibliography; sources for figures included below.

1 European Court of Auditors Annual Report 2012, 5 November 2013
   http://www.eca.europa.eu/Lists/ECADocuments/PRAR12/a13_36.EN.pdf
2 'Van Rompuy's Egg to Cost 327 million', *Flanders News.be*, 3 May 2013
   http://www.deredactie.be/cm/vrtnieuws.english/Brussels/1300503_Egg_Van_Rompuy
   'Skyrocketing Costs for Skyscraper Project', *Spiegel Online International*, 28 October 2013
   http://www.spiegel.de/international/business/cost-overruns-and-delays-plague-ecb-skyscraper-project-in-frankfurt-a-930352.html
3 Standard Eurobarometer 80, Autumn 2013
   http://ec.europa.eu/public_opinion/archives/eb/eb80/eb80_anx_en.pdf
4 Bojan Pancevski, '£1 billion for MEPs travelling circus', *Sunday Times*, 30 September 2012, p. 5.
5 The Price of a Multi-Seat European Parliament
   http://www.singleseat.eu/10.html
6 Bojan Pancevski, 'German Invasion Cuts Britons Out of Top Brussels Jobs', *Sunday Times*, 24 November 2013, p. 43.
7 *Time's Up! The case against the EU's 48-hour working week*, Open Europe, March 2009, p. 4.

8 'European Union, Trade in goods with Switzerland', Directorate General for Trade, 7 November 2013, p. 9
http://trade.ec.europa.eu/doclib/docs/2006/september/tradoc_113450.pdf

9 Camilla Cavendish, 'It's getting choppy but Britannia's 19 ships can't rule a single wave', *Sunday Times*, 22 September 2013, p. 29.

10 European Union External Action http://eeas.europa.eu/delegations/index_en.htm (Figures correct as of 22 February 2014) and European Union External Action http://eur-lex.europa.eu/budget/data/LBL2014/EN/SEC10.pdf

11 Office for National Statistics: Population by Country of Birth and Nationality Report, August 2013
http://www.ons.gov.uk/ons/rel/migration1/population-by-country-of-birth-and-nationality/2012/population-by-country-of-birth-and-nationality-report.html#tab-1--What-do-the-latest-figures-show-

12 Hansard, HL Deb, 4 February 2014, col. WA25-7.

13 'More than 3 in 4 want reduction in immigration', NatCen Social Research, 7 January 2014
http://www.natcen.ac.uk/news-media/press-releases/2014/january/more-than-3-in-4-want-reduction-in-immigration/

14 Brown, Scullion and Martin, 'Migrant Roma in the United Kingdom', October 2013
http://www.salford.ac.uk/environment-life-sciences/about/environment-and-life-sciences-news/study-finds-uk-has-200,000-roma-migrants

15 Ernst & Young's Attractiveness Survey UK 2013, pp. 4–5
http://www.ey.com/Publication/vwLUAssets/Ernst-and-Youngs-attractiveness-survey-UK-2013-No-room-for-complacency/$FILE/EY_UK_Attractiveness_2013.pdf

16 'World Investment Report 2013', United Nations Conference on Trade and Development
http://unctad.org/en/PublicationsLibrary/wir2013_en.pdf

17 UK Trade & Investment: Inward Investment Report 2012-13, p. 1
http://www.ukti.gov.uk/investintheuk/investintheukhome/item/553980.html

18 'Car manufacturing tops one million units for 2013', The Society of Motor Manufacturers and Traders, Press Release, 24 October 2013
http://www.smmt.co.uk/2013/10/car-manufacturing-tops-one-million-units-2013/

19 Office for National Statistics: Publication Tables UK Trade December 2013, 7 February 2014
http://www.ons.gov.uk/ons/taxonomy/index.html?nscl=Balance+of+Payments#tab-data-tables

20 Office for National Statistics: International Trade in Services 2012, 30 January 2014
http://www.ons.gov.uk/ons/dcp171778_351160.pdf

21 Hugo van Randwyck, EFTA or the EU (London, The Bruges Group, 2011), p. 21
    http://www.brugesgroup.com/EFTAorTheEU.pdf

22 Joana Taborda, 'Euro Area Unemployment Rate at 12% in December', Trading Economics, 31 January 2013
    http://www.tradingeconomics.com/euro-area/unemployment-rate

23 'European Union Finances 2013', HM Treasury, CM 8740, November 2013.

24 Christopher Howarth, Anna Kullmann and Pawel Swidlicki, *More for Less: Making the EU's Farm policy Work for Growth and the Environment*, Open Europe, p. 17
    http://www.openeurope.org.uk/Content/Documents/Pdfs/CAP_2012.pdf

25 'Allocation of EU structural funding across the UK', Department for Business, Innovation and Skills press release, 26 March 2013.

26 The European Economic Area and Norway Grants
    http://eeagrants.org/Who-we-are/Our-history

27 'The Swiss Contribution in brief', Federal Apartment Foreign Affairs
    http://www.contribution-enlargement.admin.ch/en/Home/The_Swiss_contribution

28 Vaughne Miller, 'How much legislation comes from Europe?', House of Commons Library Research Paper, 13 October 2010.

29 Hansard, HL Deb, 9 January 2006, col. WA10–11.

30 Will Dahlgreen, 'EU referendum: the red lines for swing voters', YouGov, 18 December 2013
    http://yougov.co.uk/news/2013/12/18/eu-referendum-red-lines-swing-voters/

31 Office for National Statistics: United Kingdom Economic Accounts Q4 2012, 27 March 2013, Table B6.

32 Ibid. Table B6B.

33 Office for National Statistics: Publication Tables UK Trade December 2013, 7 February 2014
    http://www.ons.gov.uk/ons/taxonomy/index.html?nscl=Balance+of+Payments#tab-data-tables

34 Henry Overman and Alan Winters, 'North and South', *CentrePiece*, Winter 2004.

35 'Note considering the impact of EU membership on trade and consequent welfare effects', UK Trade and Investment
    https://www.gov.uk/government/uploads/system/uploads/attachment_data/file/220968/foi_eumembership_trade.pdf

36 'World Trade Developments 2010', World Trade Organization, 2011.

37 'International Trade Statistics 2011', World Trade Organization, 2011
    http://www.wto.org/english/res_e/statis_e/its2011_e/its11_world_trade_dev_e.pdf

38 'Report highlights UK export growth in Korea', UK Trade and Investment South Korea, 4 October 2013
https://www.gov.uk/government/world-location-news/report-highlights-uk-exports-growth-in-korea

39 'World population to 2300', United Nations Department of Economic and Social Affairs, 2004
https://www.un.org/esa/population/publications/longrange2/WorldPop2300final.pdf

40 'World Trade Developments', World Trade Organization, 2011
http://www.wto.org/english/res_e/statis_e/its2011_e/its11_world_trade_dev_e.pdf

41 'Estimating the economic impact on the UK of a TTIP agreement between the EU and the US', Centre for Economic Policy Research, March 2013, pp. 32–3.

42 'Budget Report 2012 to 2014', Court of Justice of the European Union
http://eur-lex.europa.eu/budget/data/DB2014/EN/SEC04.pdf

43 'Key facts about UK financial and professional services', *TheCityUK*, 16 January 2014
https://www.thecityuk.com/research/our-work/reports-list/key-facts-about-uk-financial-and-related-professional-services/

44 ComRes: http://www.comres.co.uk/polls/Open_Europe_Final_tables_14th_December11.pdf

45 Figures provided by the European Commission directorate for Research, Innovation and Science for this book.

46 'Students in Higher Education Institutions 2011-12', Higher Education Statistics Agency.

47 '2012 UK Greenhouse Gas Emissions Final Figures', National Statistics, 4 February 2014, p. 4.

48 'Top 100 Regulations', Open Europe Briefing Note, 21 October 2013
http://www.openeurope.org.uk/Page/SingleMarket/en/live

49 'European Union Finances 2013', HM Treasury, CM 8740, November 2013.

50 Jason Cowley, 'How we pay for our richest landowners', *The New Statesman*, 19 September 2012
http://www.newstatesman.com/politics/politics/2012/09/how-we-pay-our-richest-landowners

51 'Farm business Income by type of farm in England 2012-13', Department for Environment, Food & Rural Affairs press release, 31 October 2013.

52 'CFP reform – Transferable Fishing Concessions'
ec.europa.eu/fisheries/reform/docs/tfc_en.pdf

53 'Statistics on UK Official Development Assistance', Department for International Development, 21 October 2013.

54 Juan Carlos Concepcion, 'Top 10 recipients of EU aid', Devex, 9 September 2013
https://www.devex.com/en/news/top-10-recipients-of-eu-aid/81760
55 'Annual report 2013 on the EU's Development and External Assistance policies and their implementation in 2012', European Commission, December 2013.
56 'Air passenger transport in the EU27', Eurostat news release 161/2013, 5 November 2013.
57 Eurotunnel 2012 Annual Results, 21 March 2013.
58 easyJet Annual Report and Accounts 2013, 18 November 2013.

BIBLIOGRAPHY

Bache, Ian and George, Stephen, *Politics in the European Union* (Oxford: Oxford University Press, 2006)

Bennett, Chappell, Reed and Sriskandarajah, *Trading Places: The Commonwealth Effect Revisited* (London: Royal Commonwealth Society, 2010)

Booth, Howarth, Persson and Scarpetta, *Continental Shift: Safeguarding the UK's Financial Trade in a Changing Europe* (London: Open Europe, 2011)

Booth, Howarth, Scarpetta, *Tread Carefully: The Impact and Management of EU Free Movement and Immigration Policy* (London: Open Europe, 2012)

Campbell Bannerman, David, *The Ultimate Plan B: A Positive Vision of an Independent Britain outside the European Union* (Cambridge: David Campbell Bannerman, 2011)

Charter, David, *Au Revoir, Europe: What if Britain left the EU?* (London: Biteback Publishing, 2012)

Crafts, Nicholas, *Fifty Years of Economic Growth in Western Europe* (London: World Economics, 2004)

Drew, John and Bond, Martyn (editors), *The UK & Europe: Costs, Benefits, Options. The Regent's Report 2013* (London: Regent's University, 2013)

Duff, Andrew, *On Governing Europe* (London: Policy Network and ALDE, 2012)

Eichengreen, Barry and Boltho, Angela, *The Economic Impact of European Integration* (London: Centre for Economic Policy Research, 2008)

Fram, Nicholas, *Decolonization, the Commonwealth, and British Trade 1945–2004* (Stanford: Stanford University, 2006)

Fresh Start Project, *Options for Change Green Paper: Renegotiating the UK's Relationship with the EU* (London: 2012)

Fresh Start Project, *Manifesto for Change: A New Vision for the UK in Europe* (London: 2013)

Fresh Start Project, *Mandate for Reform: Securing the Right Deal for the UK* (London: 2013)

Gaskell, Sarah and Persson, Mats, *Still Out of Control* (London: Open Europe, 2010)

Heath, Edward, *Travels: People and Places in My Life* (London: Sidgwick & Jackson, 1977)

Hennessy, Peter, *The Prime Minister: The Office and Its Holders Since 1945* (London: Penguin Books, 2001)

Hindley, Brian and Howe, Martin, *Better Off Out?* (London: The Institute of Economic Affairs, 2001)

Howarth, Kullman and Swidlicki, *More for Less: Making the EU's Farm Policy Work for Growth and the Environment* (London: Open Europe, 2012)

Ilzkovitz, Dierx, Kovacs and Sousa, *Steps Towards a Deeper Economic Integration: The Internal Market in the 21st Century* (European Economics Papers 271, 2007).

Kellner, Peter, *Worried Nationalists, Pragmatic Nationalists and Progressive Internationalists – Who Might Win a British Referendum on Europe?* (London: European Council on Foreign Relations, 2012)

Leach, Graeme, *EU Membership, What's the Bottom Line?* (London: Institute of Directors, 2000)

Mansfield, Iain, A Blueprint for Britain – Openness not Isolation (London: The Institute of Economic Affairs, 2014)

Milne, Ian, *A Cost Too Far?* (London: Civitas, The Institute for the Study of Civil Society, 2004)

Milne, Ian and Hamill, Natalie, *Withdrawal from the EU Would Not Damage our Car Industry: True or False?* (London: Civitas, The Institute for the Study of Civil Society, 2012)

Monti, Mario, *A New Strategy for the Single Market* (Brussels: European Commission, 2010)

Open Europe, *The Rise of the EU Quangos* (London: Open Europe, 2012)

Persson, Gaskell and Booth, *Time's Up! The Case Against the EU's 48-hour Working Week* (London: Open Europe, 2009)

Piris, Jean-Claude, *The Future of Europe* (Cambridge, Cambridge University Press, 2012)

Rentoul, John, *Tony Blair: Prime Minister* (Little, Brown and Company, 2001)

Reynolds, David, *The Origins of the Cold War in Europe: International Perspectives* (New Haven, Yale University Press, 1994)

Seldon, Anthony with Peter Snowdon and Daniel Collings, *Blair Unbound* (London: Simon & Schuster, 2007)

Straathof, Linders, Lejour and Moehlmann, *The Internal Market and the Dutch Economy*, (The Hague: Netherlands Bureau for Economic Policy Analysis, 2008)

Swidlicki, Ruparel, Persson and Howarth, *Off target: The Case for Bringing Regional Policy Back Home* (London: Open Europe, 2012)

Wall, Stephen, *A Stranger in Europe* (Oxford: Oxford University Press, 2008)

Winters, L. Alan, *Britain in Europe, A Survey of Quantitative Trade Studies*, (London: Centre for Economic Policy Research, 1986)

Young, Hugo, *This Blessed Plot: Britain and Europe from Churchill to Blair* (London: Papermac, 1999)

Broadcasts

European Funding, *File on 4*, BBC Radio 4, 17 July 2012

The EU Debate, *File on 4*, BBC Radio 4, 8 August 2012

Speeches

Cameron, David, EU speech at Bloomberg, 23 January 2013 (online at https://www.gov.uk/government/speeches/eu-speech-at-bloomberg)

Cameron, David, Europe speech at Chatham House, 10 November 2015 (online at https://www.gov.uk/government/speeches/prime-ministers-speech-on-europe)

GLOSSARY

Common Agricultural Policy (CAP): The European Union's system of subsidies for farmers.

Council of the European Union: Forum for national ministers to meet and take policy and legislative decisions.

Economic and Monetary Union (EMU): The system underpinning the single currency.

Euro: The European single currency shared by nineteen nations.

European Central Bank: Administers monetary policy for the countries in the single currency, based in Frankfurt.

European Commission: Executive body of the European Union responsible for administration, oversight and proposing legislation.

European Commissioner: Member of the European Commission cabinet (known as the college, comprising one representative from all twenty-eight EU member states).

European Council: EU institution where leaders from the member states meet to set policy.

European Court of Human Rights (ECtHR): Court in

Strasbourg that upholds the European Convention on Human Rights. It is not part of the European Union.

European Court of Justice (ECJ): Court based in Luxembourg that upholds and interprets EU law, comprised of one judge from each member state.

European Economic Area (EEA): Thirty-one countries (EU plus Iceland, Liechtenstein and Norway) that take part in the Single Market and adopt all relevant EU laws.

European Economic Community (EEC): Forerunner of the EU, which changed under the Maastricht Treaty of 1993.

European External Action Service: Diplomatic corps and overseas representation of the EU.

European Free Trade Association (EFTA): Four-country group (Iceland, Liechtenstein, Norway and Switzerland) originally set up with more countries including the UK in 1960 as an alternative to the EEC.

European Parliament: Elected body of the EU for revising legislative proposals comprised of 751 Members of the European Parliament (MEPs) including seventy-three from the UK.

European Union (EU): Economic and political alliance of twenty-eight nations synonymous with its main location in Brussels and built upon a series of treaties starting with the Treaty of Rome in 1957.

Four freedoms: The basis of the Single Market: the free movement of capital, goods, people and services.

Qualified Majority Voting (QMV): Method of deciding matters between ministers in the Council of the EU that attaches extra weight to bigger countries in a complicated formula.

Renegotiation: Process of consultation with the European Commission and EU member states undertaken by David Cameron to secure new membership terms for the UK ahead of the referendum.

Schengen: Name taken from a border town in Luxembourg for the European visa-free travel zone joined by twenty-six countries.

Single Market: EU customs-free internal trading area established by the Single European Act of 1986 with a Common External Tariff for imports.

Structural funds: EU aid for infrastructure projects in poorer areas.

Subsidiarity: Principle enshrined in the Maastricht Treaty that the EU shall only act when the objectives cannot be better met at national level.

ACKNOWLEDGEMENTS

Iwould like to thank Iain Dale and the whole team at Biteback Publishing for their belief and enthusiasm, particularly James Stephens for his encouragement and Hollie Teague and Olivia Beattie for their wise editing. I am grateful to John Witherow, editor of *The Times*, and Richard Beeston, our much-missed foreign editor, for providing me with the opportunity to experience the European Union at first hand as a foreign correspondent for a great newspaper. I also have a huge debt of gratitude to my immediate colleagues in *The Times* foreign news department for comradeship and support.

There are many other people to thank for their kind assistance with this book, including: Dennis Abbott, Tim Aker, Eva Baumann, Anthony Browne, David Campbell Bannerman, Stephen Cave, John Clancy, Richard Corbett, Neil Corlett, Chris Cummings, Barry Deas, Andrew Duff, Nigel Farage, Patrizio Fiorilli, Richard Freedman, Antony Gravili, Mark Gray, Martin Haworth, Joe Hennon, James Holtum, Chantal Hughes, Michael Jennings, Syed Kamall, Sony Kapoor, Helen Kearns, Graham Keeley, Maja Kocijancic, Denis MacShane, Edward McMillan-Scott, Ian Milne,

David Poyser, Fredrik Sejersted, Struan Stevenson, Ulf Sverdrup, Jonathan Todd, Gawain Towler, Marjory Van Den Broeke, Roger Waite, Jon Worth and those who talked to me off the record, as well as my former Brussels colleagues Stephen Castle, Jacki Davis, Geoff Meade, Bojan Pancevski, Nicci Smith, Ian Traynor, Bruno Waterfield and Rory Watson for the many conversations over the years. All mistakes, omissions and misunderstandings are mine. Last, but not least, I am eternally grateful to my parents, Leonard, Sheila, Liz, Ray and Mikey for their support and especially to Michelle, Leo and Kim, without whom none of this makes any sense at all.

Berlin, January 2016

For Twitter updates, please see @DavidCharter #EuropeInOrOut